100 DAYS
of
REAL FOOD
on a budget

100 DAYS
of
REAL FOOD
on a budget

Simple Tips and Tasty Recipes to Help You Cut Out Processed Food Without Breaking the Bank

LISA LEAKE

WILLIAM MORROW

An Imprint of HarperCollinsPublishers

ALSO BY LISA LEAKE

100 Days of Real Food: How We Did It, What We Learned,
and 100 Easy, Wholesome Recipes Your Family Will Love

100 Days of Real Food: Fast & Fabulous: The Easy and
Delicious Way to Cut Out Processed Food

HarperCollins books may be purchased for educational, business, or sales promotional use. For information, please email the Special Markets Department at SPsales@harpercollins.com.

FIRST EDITION

Designed by Paula Russell Szafranski

Food photography and styling by Lindsey Rose Johnson

Lifestyle photography by Daniel and Candice Lanning with The Beautiful Mess (with food styling by Tami Hardeman and Heidi Billotto and prop and wardrobe styling by Erin Rutherford with the Open Road Kitchen) except those on pages 36–38 (provided by Lisa Leake).

Library of Congress Cataloging-in-Publication Data has been applied for.

ISBN 978-0-06-266855-4

18 19 20 21 22 ID/LSC 10 9 8 7 6 5 4 3 2 1

To all the *100 Days of Real Food* readers—
We are in this together.

Thank you for your continued support and
for inspiring me with your stories!

contents

introduction

"While the response was tremendous, the feedback we most commonly heard was 'Sounds great, but too expensive.'"

After a huge wake-up call that a lot of the foods I thought were healthy were actually highly processed, I convinced my family of four we needed to completely overhaul our diets and cut out all processed food. I started a blog about our newly created "100 Days of Real Food" pledge to help draw attention to how dependent Americans have become on processed food, show that a typical suburban family could survive (and even thrive!) without it, and convince as many other people as possible to join us. And, while the response was tremendous, the feedback we most commonly heard was "Sounds great, but too expensive." So it quickly became my mission to once again prove all of this could be done, even on a strict budget.

I was originally inspired by Michael Pollan's *In Defense of Food* and, after spending months relearning how to food shop and cook for my family, it turned out to be a life-changing experience—

in more ways than one. My blog grew to the point where I knew there were thousands, even millions, of others out there just like us desperate to clean up their own family's diet, but unsure how to do it without losing their sanity. So this led to me writing not one, but two cookbooks—both of which ended up being national bestsellers!—in an effort to provide a complete easy-to-follow guide to cutting out processed food.

Meanwhile, we took our second real food challenge head-on by pledging again to eat real food, and real food only, without spending more than $125/week—less than the $167/week a family of four would receive on full SNAP (i.e., food stamp) benefits. While I would not describe this challenge as "easy"—especially at first!—we never went hungry or had to succumb to buying the dreaded processed stuff. And we never went over budget either. I learned that shopping this way wasn't as much about what foods we were in the mood for as it was about what we could afford. I also learned that by employing some simple tactics—both at the store and at home—and making the most of inexpensive ingredients, real food on a budget *could* most definitely be done.

Some of the most helpful tips that kept us on track were to plan out our meals for the week, know and use what foods we had on hand, make substitutions in recipes (to avoid going out and buying something extra), and reduce our consumption of those "nice to have" foods such as desserts, meats, and flavored beverages. I documented all the details of our budget pledge online (as well as our original pledge, which can all still be found at 100daysofrealfood.com), including all the trials and tribulations we faced along the way. And there were plenty!

The page on my blog that summarizes how we ate real food without breaking the bank has since been viewed more than one and a half million times, and I received a ton of helpful feedback from readers—so much that I knew an entire book dedicated to the topic of cost-saving tactics and budget-friendly yet delicious real food recipes would be the perfect third cookbook in my bestselling *100 Days of Real Food* series. And I'm beyond thrilled to have you here with me on this journey.

What's in This Book

The first chapter covers many different aspects of saving money in the kitchen, including how to properly set a budget, reduce your grocery bill, preserve seasonal foods, plan ahead, and reduce food waste, all of which go toward saving money. These tips and tricks are followed by one hundred real food budget-friendly recipes—seventy-five of them new, never before published—each complete with a shopping list that includes the price for every ingredient.

Sharing how much a recipe costs is nothing new, but I take a different approach to it. I've seen other budget recipes that call for 3 tablespoons of sour cream, worth only 20 cents. But when was the last time you could buy only 3 tablespoons of sour cream? I've taken the liberty of listing the *total* cost of ingredients for a recipe, whether you use them all up or not. If you don't have the extra money to spend on the rest of the sour cream container, you simply don't have it.

You'll also find my list of what I call *cheap* real foods, such as beans and bananas, that can go a long way in any home-cooked meal, followed by a set of seasonal dinner plans. If you want to dive deeper into how to define real food and fit it into your life, plus get even more recipes (including quick and easy ones), be sure to check out my first two cookbooks!

Before we jump in, though, I do want to give a brief disclaimer. Not everyone shopping for real food on a budget is dealing with the same constraints. Even though we challenged ourselves to not spend more than a family of four would receive on full SNAP benefits, I realize we still had access to more resources (reliable transportation, a variety of supermarkets close by, functioning kitchen appliances, free time at home, and so on) than some who truly need government assistance. My hope is that the information and recipes I share in the following pages will help all types of cost-conscious consumers, no matter your reasons for being on a tight budget.

How to Use the Shopping Lists in This Book

As I mentioned, prices are listed as shopping list totals for each recipe. Here's what to expect:

- Each recipe has a coordinating shopping list that shows the estimated total price to purchase all the ingredients and make the dish. Since you can't buy just one or two servings of most items, it shows you the actual cost you have to spend at the store in addition to "cost per serving."

- The shopping list prices were pulled from Publix in Charlotte, North Carolina, and will obviously vary depending on where you shop and where you live. I purposely did not gather prices from the cheapest, or the most expensive, store in our area or use coupons or sales prices. So there's a lot of potential for the total cost to be even lower than what is listed. Or, if you shop at Whole Foods or live somewhere like the Bay Area or Brooklyn (or Canada), it will likely be more expensive. And I didn't use organic prices, since that is not an official *100 Days of Real Food* rule.

- If a recipe calls for a fresh herb, such as basil, rosemary, thyme, parsley, mint, sage, or ci-

lantro, it's assumed you have it on hand, since the book contains detailed information on how to grow your own herbs easily for maximum freshness and savings (see page 33).

- If a recipe calls for a basic dried spice or ¼ cup or less of a staple pantry ingredient (see the list on page 6), it isn't added to the shopping list price on the recipe page. It's assumed you either have some basics or will make the initial investment to acquire some basics to make the recipes in this book. On the other hand, you will have leftover ingredients that aren't used in the recipe, and those are listed as well.

Staples

The ingredients below are not included in the price lists for recipes in the book, as it's assumed you will have at least ¼ cup of them on hand.

- Apple cider vinegar
- Baking powder
- Baking soda
- Balsamic vinegar
- Bay leaves
- Black pepper
- Butter
- Cayenne pepper
- Chili powder
- Coconut oil
- Curry powder (one recipe)
- Dried dill (one recipe)
- Dried oregano
- Dried thyme
- Garlic powder

- Ground allspice (one recipe)
- Ground cinnamon
- Ground coriander (one recipe)
- Ground cumin
- Ground ginger
- Ground nutmeg
- Ground turmeric (one recipe)
- Honey
- Hot sauce
- Italian seasoning
- Lemon-pepper seasoning (one recipe)
- Milk
- Mustards
- Olive oil

- Onion powder
- Paprika
- Poppy seeds (one recipe)
- Pure maple syrup
- Red pepper flakes
- Red wine vinegar
- Rice vinegar
- Salt
- Soy sauce
- Toasted sesame oil
- Vanilla extract
- White wine vinegar
- Whole wheat flour

CHAPTER 1

budgeting tips and resources

> "The key to avoiding processed food and sticking to your budget is planning ahead."

It's no secret that real, wholesome, local food has a reputation for coming with a high price tag. But thankfully, with a little know-how and ingenuity, avoiding processed food can be done on a budget! And whether you're already on board with the idea of real food or just getting started, you've come to the right place.

HOW DO WE DEFINE REAL FOOD?

Real food basically means anything not *highly* processed. Here are our rules (and there's more on how to shop for real food in my first and second cookbooks):

- No refined grains; only 100 percent whole grain

- No refined or artificial sweeteners; only honey and pure maple syrup in moderation

- Nothing out of a package that contains more than five ingredients

- No factory-farmed meat; only locally raised meat products

- No deep-fried foods

- No fast food

- Beverages to include only water, milk, occasional all-natural juices, naturally sweetened coffee and tea, and (to help the adults keep their sanity) wine and beer in moderation!

SET YOUR FOOD BUDGET

Setting a specific budget may sound like basic advice, but it's one of the most important steps and it's often overlooked, believe it or not. We've tried ourselves to go through periods of simply "not spending a lot of money," and I'm here to tell you, it doesn't work!

You need to figure out how much you can spend each week or month and come up with a reliable way to document where every single penny goes. If you don't already know how much you're currently spending on groceries, start there.

Here are four tips for structuring a grocery budget:

1. Pick a realistic budget amount.

Food budgets can range wildly for different families depending on the number of people, cost of living, and other factors. During our "*100 Days of Real Food on a Budget*" pledge back in 2010, we personally challenged ourselves to spend no more than $125/week for a family of four in Charlotte, North Carolina. I asked my Facebook followers how much they spend and heard everything from $100 to $300 a week (for a family of four), with the average coming in closer to the $150 to $250 range.

If you have no idea where to start, you should add up how much you typically spend on food each week or month (grocery store, farmers' market, any meals eaten out, and so on) by calculating an average based on credit card statements over the last six months. I personally think a weekly budget is easier to follow because you can't go too far over budget before you realize you're in trouble.

2. Decide what will be covered by the budget.

This is important! Will your grocery budget just be for food, or for household items, too? What about "extras" like alcohol, entertaining, and going out to eat? It's best to make these decisions in advance so you can track your spending accordingly.

The items our grocery budget pledge *did not* cover:

- **Eating out** We had a separate $20/week ($5/person) budget set aside for this. We usually let it accumulate so we could have one nice dinner every month or so.

- **Entertaining** We had a few instances of entertaining during our pledge, including hosting Christmas dinner, that we paid for out of a separate budget.

- **Our garden harvest** We had already purchased seeds (which are cheap!) and starter plants for a fall garden and harvested some of our lettuce and greens for "free" during our pledge.

- **Freezer stock** With the exception of meat, which didn't seem fair to eat without it counting during our challenge, we could use anything else that was already in the freezer, such as breads, homemade soups, and so on.

3. Pick a method for tracking your expenses.
There are many high-tech ways to track budgets nowadays (see page 14) and also the obvious old-school methods—which work!—such as writing down all your receipt totals and adding them up at the end of the week (or month). Years ago my husband and I used to keep tiny printed charts in our wallets so we had no excuse for forgetting to record something.

There's also the "cash envelope" method (thanks, Dave Ramsey!), in which you just dole out how much you're allowed to spend in cash. We've tried this method as well and had one envelope for groceries, another for clothes, another for entertainment, and so on. The beauty of cash is that once it's gone, it's gone!

If you aren't going to use cash (it is hard to resist all those credit card points and miles), then I suggest making a commitment that if you do go over budget, you'll deduct that amount from your new total the following week or month. And even if you do use cash, I still recommend keeping track of all your expenses, because it's important to see where your money goes.

4. Work together.
If you're part of a family, then all spenders should be responsible for helping to stay on budget. It's important to share and discuss the running totals (as well as the goal!) with the other adults and older kids in your household. I have friends who have been known to sit down their children (even those in elementary school) and present a slide show of family expenditures and goals in an effort to get everyone on the same page! Accountability is key.

IS THERE AN APP FOR THAT? OF COURSE THERE IS!

I asked my Facebook followers to share their favorite apps for grocery shopping and budget tracking, and these were some of the most popular answers:

- **YNAB (You Need a Budget)—Free 34-day trial, then $50/year.** Bank syncing and goals plus debt management software, all accessible in real time from any device. This is what we have started using for our personal finances, and we find it to be helpful.

- **EveryDollar (Dave Ramsey)—Free (with ads) or $99/year for bank syncing.** Budget from your computer, iPhone, or Android device with this tracking tool.

- **Out of Milk—Free.** Android shopping list app for creating and sharing shopping lists with friends and family.

- **Mint.com—Free (with ads).** Create budgets and bring together everything from balances and bills to your credit score and more. We have personally tried this one as well and while it pulls everything into one place for you, we felt the goal-setting features were not robust enough for our needs.

- **Flipp—Free.** Digital weekly circulars from over 800 local retailers and coupons from the brands you love so you can find the best deals in your community every week. There's a shopping list feature as well.

IT'S JUST YOUR HEALTH AT STAKE

Even if real food were to cost more than the processed stuff, there's some evidence that it might actually be worth it. "In 1960 Americans spent 17.5 percent of their income on food and 5.2 percent of national income on health care. Since then, those numbers have flipped: Spending on food has fallen to 9.9 percent, while spending on health care has climbed to 16 percent of national income."[*] It's hard to say if correlation or causation contributed to this dramatic change, but it raises the question—could you shift your budget (lower expenses in some noncritical areas) so you can **increase** the quality of your food? You might end up lowering your health care costs in the end, which would of course help your bottom line—not to mention increase your quality of life.

[*]Michael Pollan, *In Defense of Food: An Eater's Manifesto* (Penguin Press, 2008), pages 187–188.

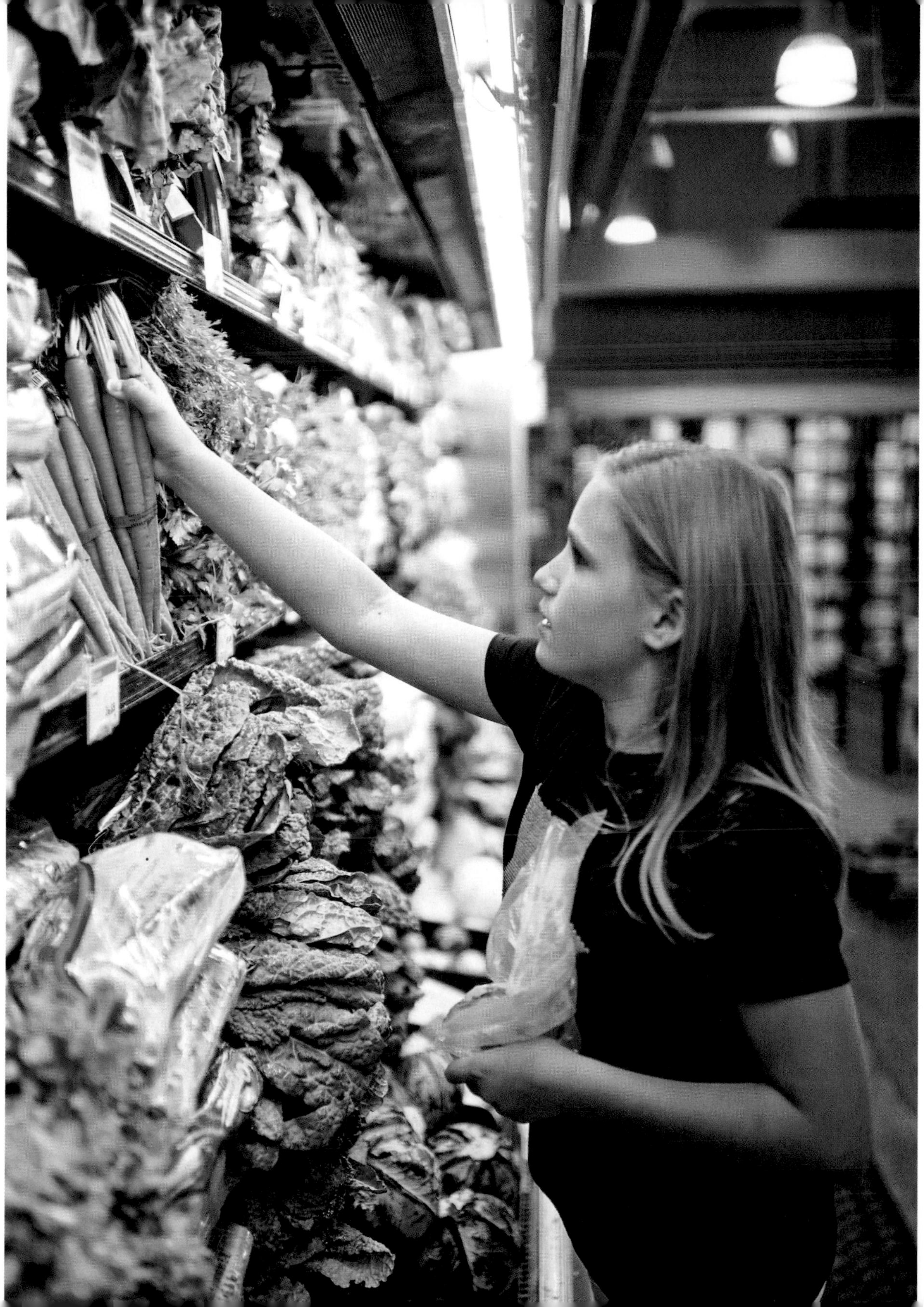

LOWER YOUR GROCERY BILL

Here are some simple ways to really stretch your dollar at the grocery store:

- **Utilize "cheap" foods (that are real, of course!).**

Put some of the least expensive real foods into your dinner rotation to help with your bottom line: bananas, beans, potatoes, cabbage, corn, frozen vegetables, watermelon, whole carrots, celery, whole wheat pasta, brown rice, and lentils.

- **Make substitutions in recipes.**

Most recipes are flexible in some way, so when possible, try using what you already have on hand (along with a little imagination) instead of going out to buy new ingredients. If you're not yet growing your own fresh herbs, try dried in their place—just use one-third of the amount called for. Use regular potatoes instead of sweet potatoes, whole milk instead of cream (in some cases, but definitely not for homemade whipped cream!), zucchini instead of bell peppers (or vice versa), chicken broth instead of veggie broth or vice versa, spinach instead of kale, rice instead of couscous, carrots instead of parsnips . . . you get the idea.

10 INGREDIENT SWAPS TO SAVE YOU MONEY

1. **Boneless, skinless chicken thighs instead of breasts >> Save $0.80 (per pound)**
   I usually prefer the flavor of chicken thighs anyway, so this one is a win-win in my opinion.

2. **Black or pinto beans for half the ground beef in tacos >> Save $1.05 (per pound)**
   I often just double my taco filling by adding 1 to 2 cans of (drained) beans to 1 pound of ground meat and doubling the spices.

3. **Lentils for half the ground beef in spaghetti >> Save $0.81 (per pound)**
   Another great way to stretch spaghetti sauce is with veggie add-ins such as mushrooms and minced carrots.

4. **Walnuts instead of pine nuts >> Save $5.50 (per 4 ounces)**
   Pine nuts are good, but boy are they pricey! Try walnuts instead for pesto and salad toppers.

5. **Cream cheese instead of goat cheese >> Save $9.59 (per 8 ounces)**
   When used as a spread on crackers or grilled sandwiches, cream cheese can be just as tasty.

6. **Frozen berries instead of fresh >> Save $2 (per pound of strawberries)**
   Especially if you're using berries in a recipe (such as a smoothie or muffins), go with frozen—I never use fresh for that purpose!

7. **Dried beans for canned >> Save $2.03 (per pound)**
   You'll have to cook them first, but it's easy and far cheaper than buying the beans in the can.

8. **Dried herbs for fresh >> Save $3 (per purchase)**
   Substitute 1 teaspoon dried herbs for 1 tablespoon fresh herbs (unless you grow your own!).

9. **Chicken or veggie broth instead of wine >> Save $2.91 (per inexpensive bottle)**
   The flavor won't be identical, but it will definitely work if you're trying to pull together a sauce on a budget.

10. **Honey for pure maple syrup >> Save $3.32 (per 8 ounces)**
    Whether it's to go in a recipe or top your morning waffles, honey is often a cheaper substitute.

• **Reduce meat and sweet treats.**

Now here's a tip that's good not only for your wallet but for your health, too. Did you know you can reap virtually the same health benefits as a vegetarian (including a lowered risk for heart disease and cancer) if you cut back to less than one serving of meat per day?[1] Meat can be a big-ticket item, especially when it's humanely raised, so experiment with stretching your ground meat dishes by cutting in diced veggies, mushrooms, and/or beans or using it as more of a side item or condiment. Even in a family of carnivores, try skipping meat altogether on occasion. And when it comes to sweet treats, make them truly special by not indulging on a daily basis. I think once a week on average is about right—your family will adjust, trust me!

• **Skip (or at least skimp on) flavored beverages.**
It's true, drinking and enjoying plain water can be an acquired taste, but flavored beverages can add up fast! If you're not quite a plain water fan, then try making your own budget flavors using the recipes on page 272. But keep giving plain water a chance—it takes time to develop a new habit!

• **Take advantage of sales and coupons.**
It's true, most coupons *are* for processed food, but that doesn't mean you should give up on coupons all together. Rather than just relying on your Sunday paper, search online for printable manufacturer coupons for national dairy brands (such as Organic Valley and Stonyfield), organic meats (such as Applegate), whole-grain pasta (such as Mueller's), brown rice (such as RiceSelect and Uncle Ben's), oils and vinegars (such as Newman's Own), and canned tomatoes and sauces (such as Muir Glen and Bertolli). It's also worthwhile to be tuned in to the sales at your supermarket so you can plan your meals around the best deals. Many grocery store chains have dedicated apps now to help keep you informed, and there's the Flipp app (see page 14), which covers multiple chains. Also check out Mambosprouts.com.

• **Buy in bulk.**
Not only is it much cheaper per pound to use the bulk bins at health food stores and some regular groceries, but you can buy the exact quantity you need. We buy all our oats, nuts, seeds, and dried beans and most of our flours in bulk each week.

• **Shop around.**
It might be convenient for your schedule but not for your wallet to buy all your groceries at one store. Especially for the nonperishable items that you routinely purchase (such as grains, nuts, seeds, flours, oils, and so on), know where to find the best prices in your area and make a special trip once a month to stock up (see chart on pages 20–23).

• **Put some thought into organic.**

Buying everything organic *can* add up fast, so I would recommend prioritizing meat and dairy, as well as the Dirty Dozen List[2] and high-risk GMO[3] crops, lists which can both easily be found online. But it's important to note that eating conventional produce is most definitely better than not eating any produce at all.

• **Rethink the TP.**

In most cases you aren't going to get your best deal on paper products, toiletries, and other personal items at the grocery store—especially if you aren't using a coupon—so I'd recommend leaving those purchases for big-box stores, warehouse clubs, or even online retailers. I'd also suggest trying to stick to your list so you can minimize impulse purchases as much as possible. I know, easier said than done (for all of us)!

• **Buy frozen.**

I wasn't always a fan of frozen produce, but that was before I learned how nutritious and inexpensive this option can be (especially in the winter!).

Frozen foods are usually picked and frozen at their peak of freshness, which beats the canned alternative and sometimes even the fresh options when they're off-season and have to be flown in from halfway across the world. So, little by little, I've found many ways to use those bags of frozen goodness, which I share on page 24.

• **Check your receipt.**

If you ever food shop when you're in a hurry, feeling hungry and irritable ("hangry"), or your kids are being especially distracting, then you might not make the most budget-conscious decisions and later regret something you purchased. It's important to know that most grocery stores do accept returns, and since I'm a pretty loyal shopper at my favorite chain, I have no problem exercising that option when necessary. One time during our budget pledge, when I was distracted by my kids, I accidentally bought a very expensive bag of organic rice that I didn't desperately need at the time. I had no problem returning the unopened rice for some much-needed cash!

SUPERMARKET COMPARISON CHART

How do grocery prices compare from store to store? Here's the breakdown where I live (Charlotte, North Carolina) as of September 2017 (after Amazon took over Whole Foods). These are not the organic prices unless noted, and since various sizes are often sold at different stores, I just did the math to give you an easy comparison.

ITEMS	ALDI	WALMART SUPER CENTER	COSTCO	TARGET	PUBLIX	KROGER	TRADER JOE'S	WHOLE FOODS MARKET
EGGS, 1 DOZEN	$0.58	$0.34	$2.99	$1.29	$1.19	$1.79	$1.19	$2.99
ORGANIC MILK, 1/2 GALLON	$2.95	$3.07	$1.15 (1 gallon size, $2.29)	$3.14	$3.69	$4.49	$3.99	$4.49
STORE BRAND BUTTER, 1 POUND	$2.29	$2.56	$2.99	$2.64	$3.15	$3.19	$2.99	$3.49
OLIVE OIL, PER OUNCE	$0.16 (16.9 oz bottle, $2.75)	$0.19 (17 oz bottle, $3.28)	$0.34 (17 oz bottle, $5.78)	$0.22 (17 oz bottle, $3.72)	$0.29 (17 oz bottle, $4.99)	$0.22 (17 oz bottle, $3.67)	$0.24 (16.9 oz bottle, $3.99)	$0.35 (16.9 oz bottle, $5.99)
BROWN RICE, PER OUNCE	$0.11* (28 oz size, $2.99)	$0.05 (16 oz size, $0.82)	$0.07 (16 oz size, $1.08)	$0.04 (16 oz size, $0.69)	$0.06 (16 oz size, $1.00)	$0.06 (16oz size, $0.89)	N/A	$0.12 (32 oz size, $3.99)

*Only organic was available.

ITEMS	ALDI	WALMART SUPER CENTER	COSTCO	TARGET	PUBLIX	KROGER	TRADER JOE'S	WHOLE FOODS MARKET
ROLLED OATS, PER OUNCE	$0.05 (42 oz size, $2.29)	$0.10 (16 oz size, $1.54)	$0.09 (32 oz size, $2.88)	$0.22 (32 oz size, $6.99)	$0.11 (16 oz size, $1.79)	$0.09 (42 oz size, $3.89)	$0.12 (32 oz size, $3.99)	$0.16 (32 oz size, $4.99)
WHOLE WHEAT FLOUR, PER POUND	N/A	$0.66 (5 lb bag, $3.28)	$0.60* (5 lb bag, $2.99)	$1.65 (2 lb bag, $3.29)	$0.86 (5 lb bag, $4.29)	$0.60 (5 lb bag, $2.99)	$0.60 (5 lb bag, $2.99)	$0.66 (5 lb bag, $3.29)
WHOLE WHEAT SPAGHETTI, 16-OZ BOX/BAG	$1.19*	$1.00	$1.14*	$2.17	$0.91	$1.00	$1.49*	$1.49*
CHICKEN BROTH, 32-OUNCE BOX	$1.19	$1.86	$1.95*	$1.42	$2.09	$1.49	$1.99*	$2.29
GROUND BEEF, 1 POUND	$2.99	$3.47	$3.29	$3.99	$3.99	$4.99	$3.99	$4.99
BONELESS, SKINLESS CHICKEN BREAST, 1 POUND	$2.29	$1.99	$2.79	$3.00 (3 lb pack, $8.99)	$3.49	$2.29	$4.99	$3.99

*Only organic was available.

ITEMS	ALDI	WALMART SUPER CENTER	COSTCO	TARGET	PUBLIX	KROGER	TRADER JOE'S	WHOLE FOODS MARKET
BANANAS, 1 POUND	$0.40	$0.28	$0.46	$0.77	$0.59	$0.55	$0.51	$0.49
CARROTS, 1 POUND BAG	$0.35 (2 lb bag, $0.69)	$0.68	$1.16	$0.85 (2 lb bag, $1.69)	$0.99	$0.99	$0.89*	$0.88*
BAKING POTATOES, 1 POUND	$0.49 (5 lb bag, $2.45)	$0.74	$0.45	$0.62 (5 lb bag, $3.12)	$1.29	$0.99	$0.76 (3 lb bag, $2.29)	$0.69
SPINACH, PER OUNCE	$0.19 (8 oz bag, $1.49)	$0.18 (16 oz bag, $2.94)	$0.31 (16 oz bag, $4.99)	$0.31 (8 oz bag, $2.49)	$0.28 (9 oz bag, $2.49)	$0.30 (16 oz bag, $4.79)	$0.33 (6 oz bag, $1.99)	$0.37 (8 oz bag, $2.99)
FROZEN PEAS, PER OUNCE	$0.06 (12 oz bag, $0.75)	$0.07 (12 oz bag, $0.84)	$0.08 (16 oz bag, $1.32)	$0.08 (12 oz bag, $0.99)	$0.11 (15 oz bag, $1.69)	$0.10 (12 oz bag, $1.19)	$0.08 (16 oz bag, $1.29)	$0.11 (12 oz bag, $1.29)
RAW CASHEWS, PER OUNCE	N/A	$0.79 (5.5 oz bag, $4.36)	N/A	$0.70 (10 oz bag, $6.99)	$0.71 (7.7 oz bag, $5.49)	$0.44 (16 oz bag, $6.99)	$0.50 (16 oz bag, $7.99)	$0.44 (per 16 oz bulk, $6.99)
RAW ALMONDS, PER OUNCE	$0.31 (14 oz bag, $4.39)	$0.43 (14 oz bag, $5.98)	$0.27 (16 oz bag, $4.33)	$0.55 (10.5 oz bag, $5.79)	$0.69 (16 oz bag, $10.99)	$0.37 (16 oz bag, $5.99)	$0.37 (16 oz bag, $5.99)	$0.94 (per 16 oz bulk, $14.99)*

*Only organic was available.

ITEMS	ALDI	WALMART SUPER CENTER	COSTCO	TARGET	PUBLIX	KROGER	TRADER JOE'S	WHOLE FOODS MARKET
PURE MAPLE SYRUP, PER OUNCE	$0.48 (12.5 oz jar, $5.99)	$0.56 (12.5 oz jar, $6.98)	$0.32 (12.5 oz jar, $3.99)	$0.60 (12 oz jar, $7.19)	$0.62 (8 oz jar, $4.99)	$0.33 (12 oz jar, $3.99)	$0.62 (8 oz jar, $4.99)	$0.60 (12.5 oz jar, $7.49)
SQUEEZE HONEY, 12 OUNCES	$2.79	$3.08	$2.50	$2.99	$2.50	$3.29	$3.49	$5.99
GRAND TOTAL	$18.76	$20.60	$22.28	$24.86	$25.98	$26.47	$28.03	$34.31

8 WAYS I USE FROZEN PRODUCE

1. Pomegranate seeds mixed into yogurt (or oatmeal).

I have to credit my daughter Sydney for this one. She loves pomegranate seeds, but let's face it, it's not the most convenient fruit to prepare. I'm reluctant to buy one and feel guilty while I watch it sit on the counter and rot, and if you buy just the fresh seeds, they don't last long. Then one day Sydney was shopping with me and noticed you could buy the seeds frozen. This is our new favorite, and they're lovely mixed into yogurt (or oatmeal)!

2. Berry mix added to cereal.

It's no secret that I love a bowl of homemade granola cereal to start my day. But it honestly isn't complete without berries on top. I love fresh berries but usually opt for frozen when they aren't in season in my area (or at least available from my continent). They're cheaper and likely more nutritious purchased frozen in the winter. And it's super easy to freeze your own (page 31), so be sure to stock up when you hit the farmers' market during the summer!

3. Blueberries or raspberries added to muffin or waffle batter (no need to thaw!).

I almost never use fresh berries when I'm making muffins or waffles—it almost seems like a waste! And since there's really no need to thaw frozen produce before adding it to the batter, it doesn't get much easier than that.

4. Peach and pineapple chunks in smoothies.

You blink and peach season is over—and it's pretty hard to find fresh organic peaches the rest of the year. Pineapple may be easier to come by, but then you have to do all that trimming and cutting. These are just some of the many reasons we almost always go for frozen produce when making smoothies at our house. Bonus: The outcome is refreshingly *cold!*

5. Frozen peas in mac and cheese (and it rhymes!).

Adding frozen peas to our mac and cheese (whether it's homemade or not) has basically become routine at our house. This is usually what we give the kids for dinner when the adults are going out, and I like how it turns their dinner into a more well-rounded one-dish meal and also quickly cools off the pasta to the perfect temp.

6. Veggie mix for stir-fry or fried rice.

Frozen veggies are sold in all sorts of blends, and I've personally become fond of the stir-fry options out there. It's hard to beat *not* having to wash and chop your veggies on a busy weeknight. And just like when I'm adding berries to my muffin or waffle batter, I don't even take the time to thaw any of them first.

7. Bananas for Banana "Ice Cream."

If you haven't tried this "trick" yet, you're *definitely* missing out! The consistency of banana ice cream is almost identical to real ice cream, and it's made by simply blending frozen bananas together with a little bit of milk. My kids absolutely *love* this one for a fun treat, and it's such a great way to use overripe bananas instead of throwing them away (or finding time to make banana bread)! Tip: Be sure to take the peels off before putting your bananas in the freezer.

8. Raspberries and/or blueberries for a colorful cake decoration.

Move over, artificially flavored/dyed sprinkles (and frosting)! We've got a better way to add color to birthday cakes. I often add frozen raspberries or blueberries on top of birthday cakes, and they're always devoured by all!

"Every time I eat mac and cheese I always add frozen peas, because it's easier than cutting up a fruit or veggie to eat on the side."

—Sienna, age 11

MINIMIZE WASTE

Throwing away food is basically throwing money down the drain. Every year the average family tosses out between $1,365 and $2,275[1] worth of uneaten food. Some of this can be blamed on the confusion about expiration date labeling; in many cases the food is mistakenly thought to be past its prime. Such a shame!

Use the following tips and you won't make the same mistakes:

- **Don't toss leftovers.**
When you cook from scratch as much as we do, leftovers are part of the system. But sometimes you're just tired of a meal after the second (or third) time, or maybe you're leaving town and can't eat it before you go. Either way, here are some options if you can't or don't want to eat your leftovers:

  - **Freeze them for a rainy day:** Most prepared foods are freezer-friendly.

  - **Reinvent your leftovers:** Turn taco filling into quesadillas, a roasted veggie side into a creamy pasta dish or veggie soup, and leftover chicken into a chicken salad sandwich or white chicken chili.

  - **Offer up a food swap:** A really good friend or neighbor may just be interested—you never know!

- **Use food scraps.**
Think twice before you throw out food scraps. The ends of your veggies or leftover chicken bones can be used to make the "Drumstick" Chicken Stock (page 233). Bread that's on its way out would be great turned into breadcrumbs or croutons. And a Parmesan cheese rind adds great flavor to vegetable soup. Get creative!

- **Understand expiration dates.**
A past expiration date can make you leery of trying a bite (or even smelling it—guilty as charged!), but expiration date confusion causes most Americans to throw away food that's perfectly good. According to the USDA and NSF (the public health and safety organization), the wording in front of the expiration date makes a difference. Check out the sidebar opposite.

THE THREE TYPES OF EXPIRATION DATES

1. **Use by.** This wording is more about food safety than any of the others. It's commonly found on fresh foods like dairy and meat products. You should either use or freeze items by this date, and obviously not purchase any food items past this date.

2. **Best before / Best if used by.** This statement is more about quality than anything else. It's simply a guideline to let you know how long the product will remain at peak quality and freshness. It's generally still safe to consume the product after that date.

3. **Sell by / Packed on.** These dates are there to let the store know how long to display a product for sale. It's a good idea to purchase products on or before the "sell by" date, but you can definitely consume foods past that date.

• Make a plan—and stick to it!

Meal plans are an important part of budgeting. Finding yourself out of the house at dinnertime with starving kids in the backseat and no plan can easily end up costing you. And don't even get me started on how much money you can waste impulse shopping at the grocery store when you're hungry and don't know what to buy. While we all certainly have our "off" days, make a plan—and do your best to stick to it! See more on this topic on page 39.

• Know and use what you have on hand.

The first step in coming up with that beloved meal plan for the week should always be to look through your fridge and see what needs to be eaten (or preserved) before it spoils. One of my favorite things about regularly making and using dinner plans for my family is that we have very little uneaten food leftover at the end of the week, because with a plan, you only buy what you need and intend to use! And even if you don't plan your meals, you should still conduct regular checks of your fridge and make notes (mental or written) on what needs to be eaten soon. I find a good ol' handwritten sticky note on the fridge door is helpful if you have other family members who might come looking for a snack. And even cutting up fruit and veggies—making them appealing and ready to eat—helps prevent food from going to waste.

• Use reusables.

Now, when it comes to storing and enjoying all that yummy homemade food you've prepared, save big by cutting back on the expense of single-use items in favor of reusables.

• Reusable water bottle >> Plastic bottled water
I'm not about to claim I never buy bottled water, but I do try hard to avoid it. One incentive is being able to use my insulated Thermos bottle that keeps water cold for up to twelve hours (I'm a huge fan of ice-cold water!). I love to bring it empty to the airport and fill it up after passing through security.

- **Reusable storage containers >> Plastic re-sealable bags** Invest in some sturdy storage containers for both home and school/work and you'll be more likely to skip the plastic baggies for your sandwich on the go. We love to use large glass jars to store all our bulk items in as well.

- **Reusable dinner plates >> Paper plates** I know it's tempting, but—unless you're hosting a party—sticking to plates you can wash and reuse is a simple way to save some cash.

- **Cloth dish rags >> Paper towels** Buy some washable dish cloths for spills and pair them with your favorite counter spray for cleaning surfaces. Have enough on hand to switch them out every day or two so they never get too "germy."

- **Cloth napkins >> Paper napkins** Saying goodbye to paper napkins was something I considered for a long time before I actually did it. Once we finally made the switch (and I realized how easy it was), I couldn't believe I'd waited so long. More about our how we've made this work on the next page.

HOW WE FINALLY DITCHED PAPER NAPKINS

The first step was to clear out a drawer in the kitchen to store our new cloth napkins (they take up a lot more room than a little stack of paper ones). I dedicated a day to ridding our kitchen of some items we weren't really using, ordered some attractive napkins that appeared to be wrinkle-free (because I wasn't about to pretend I'd be ironing them, ha ha—I love the sets from Anthropologie), and came up with a new routine. We decided we didn't need a "fresh" napkin for every single meal, so in between uses we just hang our colorful new napkins on the back of our chairs. I also placed a basket on the floor of our pantry to collect the dirty ones (along with dirty dish towels and rags) until enough accumulate to be a full load in the wash. I must say that this new routine is easy peasy—and not only do we save money by not buying paper napkins, we also really enjoy the more upscale feel of using *real* napkins at the table! My eleven-year-old likes to make a big show of how much she disapproves of using paper napkins now (which still occasionally happens when we have friends over). It's official—she's spoiled by our nice cloth napkins!

"I must say that this new routine is easy peasy—and not only do we save money by not buying paper napkins, we also really enjoy the more upscale feel of using real napkins at the table!"

GROW AND PRESERVE SEASONAL FOODS

If you want local blueberries in your homemade granola cereal in December, then it's up to you to freeze enough in the summer to last until the next berry season. Not only is it more affordable to preserve local produce such as blueberries when they're at their peak, but the taste is far superior to the packaged frozen blueberries from the store. Preserving your farmers' market finds is the best way to eat local all year long.

4 Ways to Preserve Fresh Berries for the Winter

1. Freeze berries in containers.

Freeze unwashed berries in batches on a baking sheet, then transfer them to a large zip-top bag or other freezerproof container. Give the frozen berries a quick rinse before adding to things like cereal, smoothies, plain yogurt, pancakes, or homemade muffins. Frozen berries can also be used to make recipes such as jams and pie without having to thaw.

2. Can some jam.

Make homemade jam that you either freeze or can. Be sure to check out my online "How to Can Some Jam" tutorial for a berry-honey jam recipe that doesn't call for refined sugar or pectin (www.100daysofrealfood/canning).

3. Dehydrate berries.

Dehydrate berries whole or puree them first to make homemade fruit leathers (see page 151). You can use either a dedicated dehydrator or a regular oven at a very low temperature. Dehydrated whole berries can be eaten as a snack or added to foods like granola, oatmeal, or yogurt.

4. Freeze berries in recipes.

Make complete dishes with fresh berries and then freeze them. Some examples are blueberry muffins, raspberry pancakes, mixed berry smoothies, berry sauce (for yogurt), and blackberry pie. You can freeze finished recipes like pancakes using the baking sheet freezer method mentioned in #1 (page 31), or you can freeze them together separated by sheets of wax paper.

Growing Fresh Herbs Can Save You Money

Spending two or three bucks on a pack of fresh herbs at the grocery store every time you need a sprig of thyme or a few mint leaves can add up quickly! Luckily, growing them yourself couldn't be any easier. If you've been pondering the idea of starting your own edible garden, this is honestly the perfect way to start.

Obviously everyone's cooking habits are different, but here are some estimates (not including tax, just to keep things simple) that show how much you can save.

COST COMPARISON

Cost of Grocery Store Herb Packs
2X/Month = $52.56/year
3X/Month = $78.84/year
4X/Month = $105.12/year
5X/Month = $131.40/year
6X/Month = $157.68/year

Cost of Herb Plants
5 different plants = $18.40/year
6 different plants = $22.08/year
7 different plants = $25.76/year

Cost of Herb Seed Packets
5 different packs = $7.50/year
6 different packs = $9.00/year
7 different packs = $10.50/year

Since some herbs only have to be planted once and others will die back (or die altogether) at the end of the season, it's hard to completely eliminate the need to buy fresh herbs from the grocery store ever again. But as you can see, the savings can really add up no matter how often you use them!

WHEN TO GROW FRESH HERBS

I can tell you from experience that herbs are one of the easiest things I've ever attempted to grow. They are thankfully hard to mess up! Here's some of what I've learned during my attempts in Charlotte, North Carolina.

YEAR-ROUND HERBS

You only have to plant these once; they're usually hardy enough to last through the winter.

Rosemary

Thyme

Oregano (depends on the winter if they'll hold up)

WARM-WEATHER HERBS

Plant in the spring; some may come back for another season. This is just a partial list of my personal favorites, and most can be planted from seed.

Basil

Sage

Mint (recommended in a pot—more on that at right)

Flat-leaf parsley

Dill

Tarragon

COOL-WEATHER HERBS

This one can be a little tricky . . . not so great in super-cold or super-hot weather, so more early spring or late fall is best.

Cilantro (the seed is called coriander)

GENERAL GROWING TIPS

- **Most herbs will bolt.**
Bolt, flower, go to seed—all basically the same thing. When your basil starts to sprout little flowers (where the seeds form), simply pinch those little stalks off at the top to keep the plant thriving.

Some warm-weather herbs may last more than one season if you're trimming as needed, but the basic rule of thumb is this: When the herb no longer tastes good, it's done.

- **Plant mint in a pot!**
I learned this lesson the hard way, so hopefully I can prevent you from making the same mistake. Many years ago when I was home from college for the summer I asked my parents if I could try my hand at planting a few fresh herbs in their yard. They said yes, and before I knew it (much to their dismay), my mint had completely taken over! No matter how much I tried to keep it from spreading, the plant clearly had its mind made up about procreating. This one will go wild—literally—so keep it at bay in a pot.

- **Give most a chance to last through winter.**
With the exception of basil, here in North Carolina many of the warm-weather herbs could very well come back for another season or two. So before you pull yours up and toss them in the trash (or compost) at the end of the summer, just let them be and give them a chance to come back the next year.

- **Outdoors is best.**
Herbs might survive for a short time inside, but to really thrive they need the outdoor, unfiltered sun. If you must plant inside, make sure to place herbs near a sunny window, and consider giving them outside time a couple days a week.

- **Don't forget the TLC.**

As with any sun-loving plant, herbs of course need to be planted in good soil in a sunny spot and watered as needed (every two or three days, or when they start to look droopy and the soil feels dry). You can also add a little organic fertilizer (I like PlantTone) if you really want to give them an extra good chance. That's the same stuff I use in my vegetable garden, but I don't find it necessary when it comes to growing herbs.

There's really not a lot to lose when it comes to planting herbs, I promise! It's a great way to get your feet wet if you want to try growing your own food.

"Growing fresh herbs is fun and easy to do because you get to take care of your very own plant!"

—Sydney, age 13

STOCK A BASIC REAL FOOD KITCHEN

In 2017 we joined the exciting world of tiny houses—talk about living on a budget! Now, we don't live in our 300-square-foot tiny house full-time, but since it was the only way we could afford a getaway in the nearby North Carolina moun-

tains (where it's *much* cooler and less humid in the summer), we decided to take the plunge.

Stocking our tiny house kitchen turned out to be a fun experiment in determining the most important kitchen tools I'd need in order to cook from scratch there. We have all sorts of fun kitchen gadgets at home that get only occasional use—such as our panini grill and waffle cone maker—but of course there's no room for luxuries like that in a tiny house kitchen, so I am sharing what I came up with here and on the next page. You can learn more about our tiny house and take the video tour here: www.100daysofrealfood.com/tiny-house/.

KITCHEN TOOLS AND APPLIANCES IN OUR TINY HOUSE

Cooking and Prep Tools

- Pots and pans: 3 pots (1-quart, 2-quart, 4-quart) and 3 pans (8-inch skillet, 10-inch skillet, 3-quart sauté pan)—all factory seconds!

- Cast-iron skillet: Great for homemade tortillas

- Cutting boards: A combo of wood and plastic, all from Ikea

- Good set of knives

- Kitchen shears

- Colander and small strainer

- Salad spinner: I honestly didn't even own a salad spinner before cutting out processed food, and now I use it all the time for lettuce, greens, and even fresh herbs.

- Steamer basket

- Set of graduated mixing bowls (the big ones can double as serving bowls)

Baking Dishes

- Large and small casserole dishes: Also from Ikea

- Pie plate: We use this most often to make quiche

- Small baking sheet

- Cooling rack—great for cooling baked goods, but we also use ours for making oven-cooked bacon.

- Muffin pan

- Loaf pan

"Stocking our tiny house kitchen turned out to be a fun experiment . . ."

Cooking Utensils

- Basic cooking spatulas/spoons
- Rubber spatulas
- Small whisk
- Tongs
- Roux spoon

Other Small Kitchen Tools

- Box-style cheese grater
- Carrot peeler
- Small zester/Microplane grater
- Silicone brush
- Can opener
- Potato brush

- Stainless-steel measuring spoons and cups
- Glass measuring cups (for liquids): 1-cup and 2-cup sizes
- Lemon juicer
- Apple slicer
- Small ice cream scoop: Great for spooning muffin, cupcake, and cookie batter
- Wine opener—of course!
- Meat thermometer
- Small rolling pin

Small Appliances

- Electric hand mixer
- Slow cooker: Cannot live without this one
- Basic toaster
- Immersion hand blender
- Waffle maker: This was our one "not really necessary" splurge, but the girls talked me into getting a Belgian waffle maker (ours at home is just a regular waffle maker, not Belgian), and I liked the idea of having something special like this that we enjoy only in the mountains!
- Small espresso maker

Miscellaneous Items

- Handful of jelly jars and lids
- A couple of cookie cutters—I use these when making biscuits
- Milk frother: So I can make the Maple Mocha recipe from my blog

Whether you live in a small space or need help figuring out what items are most critical when it comes to making real food (or even need ideas for a wedding registry), this list is a good place to start.

ALWAYS HAVE A PLAN

I often say the key to avoiding processed food is planning ahead. It's also the key to sticking to your budget. I plan five or six dinners a week for our family, incorporating leftovers at least one night to give me a break from cooking, and leaving one or two nights to be determined. Plans change and sometimes life just gets in the way, so it's nice not to have ingredients that'll go to waste if I wasn't able to make a good dinner more than five or six nights in a week.

I also love to plan on doubling some recipes as well. The extra cost and time involved are often minimal, and then you can eat what's left for lunch or stash it away in your freezer for a rainy day. This is one of the reasons we bought an extra freezer when we first decided to cut out processed food.

THREE TRAVEL TIPS

I save money by planning ahead not only at home but also when I'm traveling.

1. **Forget the expensive breakfast buffet.** I always bring a bag of my homemade granola when staying in hotels. The staff often just gives me a glass of milk (along with a bowl and a spoon) at no charge!

2. **When traveling during the lunch or dinner hour I always bring my own food.** I'll either make (and sometimes freeze) the bean and veggie burritos from my *Fast & Fabulous* cookbook, make BLTs on frozen bread, or just throw together a PB&J—frozen items usually thaw out by the time we're ready to eat. Unless it's a liquid—or resembles a liquid, such as yogurt and applesauce—you *can* bring food through security.

3. **And as I already mentioned, I bring an empty insulated water bottle to the airport** and just fill it up after going through security. I try to buy as few things as possible when subjected to airport prices!

MEAL PLAN: WINTER

A seven-day real-food dinner plan for a family of four and coordinating shopping list with pricing.

MENU

Sunday: Swedish Meatballs (page 204, double the recipe) over egg noodles plus a side salad

Monday: Chicken Burrito Bowls (page 80)

Tuesday: Leftover Swedish meatballs with steamed green beans

Wednesday: Zucchini and Black Bean Enchiladas (page 211)

Thursday: Baked Shells with Ricotta and Marinara (page 184) with Shredded Brussels Sprouts (page 123, double the recipe)

Friday: Apple-Glazed Pork Chops (page 176) with baked russet or sweet potatoes and leftover shredded Brussels sprouts

Saturday: Breadcrumb-Roasted Chicken (page 212) with leftover baked shells with ricotta and marinara plus a side salad

SHOPPING LIST

PRODUCE

Two 8-ounce bags Brussels sprouts	$5.58
Two 1-pound bags carrots	$1.98
1 pound green beans	$2.49
1 zucchini	$1.27
One 5-ounce bag/box spinach or mixed greens (for 2 side salads)	$2.49
2 tomatoes (½ pound)	$0.89
1 garlic head	$0.50
3 small onions	$1.68
2 pounds russet or sweet potatoes	$2.58
1 lime	$0.25
1 lemon	$0.65
1 apple	$0.75

DAIRY/EGGS

½ pint heavy cream	$2.29
One 8-ounce container sour cream	$0.99
One 8-ounce box butter	$2.69
Two 8-ounce blocks Monterey Jack cheese	$7.78
One 15-ounce container ricotta cheese	$2.49
One 8-ounce block mozzarella cheese	$3.89
One 6-ounce tub freshly grated Parmesan cheese	$3.99

MEAT

2½ pounds boneless, skinless chicken breasts	$8.73
1 pound thin, boneless pork chops	$5.29
1 pound ground pork	$2.50
1 pound ground beef	$4.00

FROZEN

One 15-ounce bag frozen corn	$1.69

INTERIOR AISLES: DRY/CANNED/GRAINS

One 16-ounce bag brown rice	$1.00
One 16-ounce box whole wheat pasta shells	$1.69
One 12-ounce bag whole wheat egg noodles	$2.39
Two 8-count packages whole-grain corn tortillas	$3.78
One 2-pound bag whole wheat flour	$3.49
One 15-ounce canister whole wheat breadcrumbs	$2.89
Three 14.5-ounce cans broth (chicken or veggie)	$4.11
One 15-ounce can black beans	$0.95
One 15-ounce can plain tomato sauce	$1.13
One 28-ounce can crushed tomatoes	$1.28
One 11.5-ounce bottle apple juice	$1.89
TOTAL COST	**$92.04**

PANTRY CHECKLIST

Allspice
Balsamic vinegar
Black pepper
Cayenne pepper
Chili powder
Cilantro (garden)
Cumin
Italian seasoning
Olive oil
Oregano flakes
Parsley (garden)
Sage leaves (garden)
Salt
Soy sauce
Thyme (garden)

MEAL PLAN: SPRING

A seven-day real-food dinner plan for a family of four and coordinating shopping list with pricing.

MENU

Sunday: Deconstructed Spring Roll Bowls (with shrimp, page 94)

Monday: Weeknight Tandoori Chicken (page 208)

Tuesday: Slow Cooker Carrot Curry Soup (page 223) with Kale and Bacon–Stuffed Potatoes (page 121, double the recipe)

Wednesday: Creamy Braised Pork Chops (page 191) with leftover kale and bacon–stuffed potatoes and roasted broccoli (double quantity, roasted at 450°F for 25 to 30 minutes)

Thursday: Baked Sweet Potato Taquitos (page 207, double the recipe) with a simple spinach salad

Friday: Jason's Carne Asada (served by itself, page 183) with leftover taquitos and leftover roasted broccoli

Saturday: Easy Chicken Scaloppine (page 200) over brown rice with a simple spinach salad

SHOPPING LIST

PRODUCE

1 cucumber	$0.50
1 pound carrots	$0.99
2 pounds broccoli	$5.00
2 jalapeño peppers	$0.62
1 bunch kale	$1.99
Two 5-ounce bags fresh spinach	$4.98
1 garlic head	$0.50
1 onion	$0.85
4 russet potatoes	$3.44
2 small sweet potatoes	$1.30
1 lemon	$0.65
2 limes	$0.50
1 mango	$1.66

DAIRY/EGGS

½ pint heavy cream	$2.29
One 5.3-ounce container plain yogurt	$1.00
One 16-ounce container sour cream	$1.33
One 8-ounce box butter	$2.69
One 8-ounce block Monterey Jack cheese	$3.89
One 6-ounce tub freshly grated Parmesan cheese	$3.99

MEAT

1 pound boneless, skinless chicken breasts	$3.49
1½ pounds boneless, skinless chicken thighs	$4.04
1B/e pounds thin, boneless pork chops	$6.61
1B/c pounds flank steak	$10.49
One 8-ounce package bacon	$4.19

FROZEN

1 pound shrimp (purchase frozen)	$8.99
One 15-ounce bag frozen corn kernels	$1.69

INTERIOR AISLES: DRY/CANNED/GRAINS

One 16-ounce bag brown rice	$1.00
One 8-ounce bag/box brown rice noodles, Asian style	$4.29
Five 8-count packages whole-grain corn tortillas	$9.45
One 2-pound bag whole wheat flour	$3.49
One 16-ounce jar peanut butter	$2.67
One 16-ounce canister roasted, salted peanuts	$3.49
Two 13.5-ounce cans coconut milk	$4.98
One 8-ounce can plain tomato sauce	$0.27
One 32-ounce can/box vegetable or chicken broth	$2.09
Two 15-ounce cans black beans	$1.90
TOTAL COST	**$110.80**

PANTRY CHECKLIST

Black pepper
Cayenne pepper
Cilantro (garden)
Coriander
Cumin
Curry powder
Garlic powder
Ginger
Mint (garden)
Olive oil
Onion powder
Oregano flakes
Paprika
Rice vinegar
Salt
Soy sauce
Toasted sesame oil

MEAL PLAN: SUMMER

A seven-day real-food dinner plan for a family of four and coordinating shopping list with pricing.

MENU

Sunday: Rainbow Salad with Salmon (page 110) with brown rice on the side

Monday: Fast-Food Chicken Nuggets (page 186) with Green Apple–Cucumber Slaw (page 113) and Campfire Potatoes (page 114)

Tuesday: Sausage and Pepper Tacos (page 179) with corn on the cob

Wednesday: Sydney's Veggie Cream Pasta (page 175, double the recipe) with roasted or grilled pork tenderloin

Thursday: Asian Chicken Lettuce Cups (page 172) with Coconut Rice (page 130)

Friday: Leftover veggie cream pasta with a side salad and Garlic Toast (page 143)

Saturday: Portobello Tartine (page 96) with Simple Zucchini Soup (page 90)

LISA'S TIP: For a Simple Roasted Pork Tenderloin recipe, we love the one on page 228 in my *Fast & Fabulous* cookbook. You mix together 1 teaspoon paprika, ½ teaspoon garlic powder, ½ teaspoon onion powder, ½ teaspoon salt, ⅛ teaspoon ground black pepper, and 1 tablespoon olive oil and rub the tenderloin with it. Bake at 425°F until the pork is cooked all the way through (no longer pink and to an internal temperature of 160°F for medium), 25 to 35 minutes.

SHOPPING LIST

PRODUCE

1 cucumber	$0.50
4 ears corn	$2.40
One 16-ounce bag radishes	$1.69
3 pounds zucchini	$5.07
3 green bell peppers	$2.97
2 jalapeño peppers	$0.62
One 6-ounce package portobello caps	$3.69
Two 5-ounce bags/boxes mixed salad greens	$5.98
1 head Bibb or iceberg lettuce	$0.99
¼ pound fresh ginger	$1.26
1 garlic head	$0.50
1 bunch green onions	$0.89
1 onion (8 ounces)	$0.85
1 large sweet potato	$0.65
One 28-ounce bag small (new) potatoes	$4.49
1 mango	$1.66
2 Granny Smith apples	$2.29
1 lime	$0.25

DAIRY/EGGS

1 pint heavy cream	$3.04
One 16-ounce container sour cream	$1.33
One 8-ounce box butter	$2.69
One 8-ounce block Monterey Jack cheese	$3.89
One 6-ounce tub freshly grated Parmesan	$3.99
One 8-ounce pack sliced provolone cheese	$3.39
1 dozen eggs	$1.19

MEAT/SEAFOOD

1½ pounds boneless, skinless chicken breasts	$5.24
1½ pounds pork tenderloin	$7.49
One 20-ounce pack kielbasa or bratwurst sausage links (raw)	$5.99
¾ pound wild-caught salmon	$7.49

INTERIOR AISLES: DRY/CANNED/GRAINS

One 16-ounce bag brown rice	$1.00
One 16-ounce box whole wheat fettuccine noodles	$2.99
One 8-count package whole-grain corn tortillas	$1.89
One 2-pound bag whole wheat flour	$3.49
1 loaf good-quality 100% whole wheat bread	$4.99
One 1-ounce container toasted sesame seeds	$3.29
One 32-ounce box veggie or chicken broth	$2.09
One 14.5-ounce can veggie or chicken broth	$1.37
One 13.5-ounce can coconut milk	$1.49
One 16-ounce jar pickles	$1.99
TOTAL COST	**$105.18**

PANTRY AND FRIDGE CHECKLIST

Apple cider vinegar
Balsamic vinegar
Basil (garden)
Black pepper
Cilantro (garden)
Coconut oil
Dry mustard
Garlic powder
Honey
Olive oil
Oregano flakes
Paprika
Parsley, if using (garden)
Red pepper flakes
Rice vinegar
Salt
Soy sauce
Toasted sesame oil

MEAL PLAN: FALL

A seven-day real-food dinner plan for a family of four and coordinating shopping list with pricing.

MENU

Sunday: Easy Walnut-Crusted Salmon (page 167) with Sheet Pan Brussels Sprouts and Potatoes (page 126)

Monday: Easy Chinese Chicken (page 168, double the recipe) with Maple-Roasted Sweet Potatoes and Carrots (page 131, double the recipe) and Coconut Rice (page 130, double the recipe)

Tuesday: Spaghetti Squash Carbonara (page 196) with Melt-in-Your-Mouth Cream Biscuits (page 118, double the recipe) and a spinach side salad

Wednesday: Leftover Chinese chicken, maple-roasted veggies, and coconut rice

Thursday: Black Olive and Tomato Frittata (page 59) with leftover cream biscuits and roasted eggplant (thinly sliced, seasoned with salt, pepper, and olive oil, and roasted at 400°F until golden brown)

Friday: Slow Cooker Shredded Moo Shu Pork (page 229, use a 3½- to 4-pound roast) with whole wheat tortillas, shredded cabbage mix (slaw), and baked sweet potatoes on the side

Saturday: Leftover moo shu pork with Stir-Fry Broccoli (page 129) and brown rice

SHOPPING LIST

PRODUCE

One 16-ounce bag + 8-ounce bag Brussels sprouts	$7.28
Two 1-pound bags carrots	$1.98
1 pound broccoli	$2.50
1 pound eggplant	$1.99
2¼-pound spaghetti squash	$4.48
One 5-ounce bag fresh spinach	$2.49
One 16-ounce bag shredded cabbage	$1.79
½ pound Roma (plum) tomatoes (2)	$1.00
2 garlic heads	$1.00
¼ pound fresh ginger	$1.26
1 bunch green onions	$0.89
2 small onions	$1.12
One 28-ounce bag fingerling or new potatoes	$4.49
3 pounds sweet potatoes	$4.50

DAIRY/EGGS

1 pint + ½ pint heavy cream	$5.33
Two 13.5-ounce cans coconut milk	$2.98
1 dozen eggs	$1.19
One 6-ounce tub freshly grated Parmesan	$3.99

MEAT/SEAFOOD

3 pounds boneless, skinless chicken thighs	$8.06
4 pounds pork shoulder	$13.16
1 pound wild-caught salmon	$9.99
One 8-ounce package bacon	$4.19

INTERIOR AISLES: DRY/CANNED/GRAINS

One 16-ounce bag brown rice	$1.00
Two 16-ounce bags whole wheat tortillas	$4.70
One 2-pound bag whole wheat flour	$3.49
One 3-pound bag whole wheat pastry flour	$3.69
One 15-ounce canister whole wheat breadcrumbs	$2.89
One 4-ounce bag chopped walnuts	$2.99
One 1-ounce container toasted sesame seeds	$3.29
One 3.8-ounce can black olives	$1.59
One 15-ounce bottle soy sauce	$2.49
One 16-ounce jar peanut butter	$2.67
TOTAL COST	**$114.46**

PANTRY CHECKLIST

Apple cider vinegar
Baking powder
Black pepper
Cinnamon
Coconut oil
Dijon mustard, or regular mustard
Ground ginger
Honey
Maple syrup
Olive oil
Paprika
Red pepper flakes
Rice vinegar
Salt
Toasted sesame oil
Turmeric

FULL MEAL PLAN TEMPLATE

DAY	BREAKFAST	LUNCH	SNACK	DINNER
Sunday				
Monday				
Tuesday				
Wednesday				
Thursday				
Friday				
Saturday				

Recipes that should be made in advance over the weekend for the upcoming week:

Recipe 1:

Recipe 2:

Recipe 3:

SHOPPING LIST TEMPLATE

PRODUCE

Qty.	Item

INTERIOR AISLES: DRY / CANNED / GRAINS

Qty.	Item

MEAT / SEAFOOD

Qty.	Item

FROZEN

Qty.	Item

BULK / MISC / OTHER

Qty.	Item

DAIRY / EGGS

Qty.	Item

PANTRY CHECKLIST (ITEMS YOU HAVE ON HAND)

Item	Item
☐	☐
☐	☐
☐	☐
☐	☐
☐	☐
☐	☐
☐	☐
☐	☐

breakfast

breakfast recipes

The Best Waffles

My middle schooler is a waffle-eating machine. I'll often make one big double batch over the weekend that she'll demolish in no time. She's a growing girl, so she'll eat anywhere between 2½ to 3 waffles (plus fresh fruit—my requirement!) in one sitting. I let her have at it while they're fresh on Sunday morning and then I freeze the rest for her to heat up before school. The whole bag is usually gone by week's end.

1. Preheat the waffle iron.

2. In a large bowl, whisk together the flour, baking powder, and salt. In a separate large bowl, with an electric mixer, beat the egg whites until they form soft peaks. Melt the butter and syrup together (I prefer to do this in a small pot on the stove).

3. Make a well (hole) in the center of the flour mixture and use a fork to stir in the milk, egg yolks, and melted butter/syrup mixture until well combined. Lumps in the batter are okay. Carefully fold in the egg whites using a rubber spatula.

4. Cook in the waffle iron according to the manufacturer's directions. Serve warm with warm maple syrup and fresh fruit—my daughter prefers blueberries with this one!

Difficulty: Medium
Prep time: 15 minutes
Cook time: 20 minutes (cooked in batches)
Makes 8 to 10 regular (not Belgian) waffles
Special tools: Electric waffle iron

VEGETARIAN
NUT-FREE
FREEZER-FRIENDLY

1¾ cups whole wheat flour (pastry or regular)
2 teaspoons baking powder
½ teaspoon salt
3 eggs, separated
5 tablespoons butter
1 tablespoon pure maple syrup (or honey)
1¼ cups milk

Suggested accompaniments: Fresh fruit and pure maple syrup

SHOPPING LIST		PANTRY AND FRIDGE CHECKLIST
One 3-pound bag whole wheat pastry flour	$3.69	2 teaspoons baking powder
Half dozen eggs	$0.85	Salt
One 8-ounce box butter	$2.69	1 tablespoon pure maple syrup or honey
1 pint milk	$0.99	
TOTAL	**$8.22**	**INGREDIENTS LEFT OVER**
COST PER SERVING	**$0.82**	Whole wheat pastry flour
		Eggs
		Butter
		Milk

"These waffles really are the best waffles in the whole entire world, and I always beg my mom to make them!"

—Sydney, age 13

Breakfast Smoothie Bowl

Difficulty: Easy
Prep time: 10 to 15 minutes
Cook time: N/A
Makes 3 to 4 servings
Special tools: Blender

GLUTEN-FREE (IF GLUTEN-FREE OATS ARE USED)
DAIRY-FREE
VEGETARIAN
NUT-FREE (IF PEANUT BUTTER IS OMITTED)
FREEZER-FRIENDLY (IF THAWED SLIGHTLY TO RETURN ORIGINAL CONSISTENCY BEFORE EATING)

2 cups spinach

1⅓ cups coconut water

4 bananas, frozen

1 cup frozen sliced peaches

⅓ cup peanut butter

⅓ cup rolled oats

⅓ cup raw pepitas (hulled pumpkin seeds)

My daughters are such big fans of the Banana "Ice Cream" recipe from my second cookbook that they sometimes eat it for breakfast. So, inspired by all the smoothie bowl recipes sweeping the Internet, we decided to add some extras to their beloved Banana "Ice Cream" breakfast to make it more of a complete meal.

1. In a blender, combine the spinach, coconut water, bananas, peaches, and peanut butter and blend until smooth. Spoon into bowls.

2. In a small, dry skillet, toast the oats and pumpkin seeds over medium heat, stirring frequently, until golden brown, 2 to 3 minutes. Sprinkle on top of the smoothie bowls and serve.

SHOPPING LIST		PANTRY AND FRIDGE CHECKLIST
One 5-ounce bag spinach	$2.49	N/A
One 11.3-ounce can coconut water	$0.59	**INGREDIENTS LEFT OVER**
4 bananas	$0.80	Spinach
One 20-ounce bag frozen sliced peaches	$3.85	Coconut water
One 18-ounce jar peanut butter	$2.67	Peaches
¼ pound rolled oats	$0.45	Peanut butter
One 4.6-ounce bag raw pepitas	$2.99	Pepitas
TOTAL	**$4.34**	
COST PER SERVING	**$3.46**	

LISA'S TIPS: As I mentioned on page 25, it's best to freeze bananas with the peel off—that's a mistake you'll only make once! The riper they are when you freeze them, the sweeter they'll be. And buying peaches already frozen is a budget-friendly option at any time of year.

Black Olive and Tomato Frittata

I never would've thought to put olives on an omelet or frittata until we tried it while on a trip to Morocco. With olive trees in abundance in the area, olives showed up in a variety of dishes, and it really opened my eyes to the many ways you can cook with them (not just eat them as a snack or appetizer). I'll never look at olives the same again!

1. Preheat the oven to 375°F.

2. In a large sauté pan, heat the olive oil over medium-low heat. Add the onion, paprika, turmeric, salt, and pepper to taste and cook until the onions soften, stirring often, 4 to 5 minutes.

3. Take the pan off the heat, spread the onions into even layer, pour in the eggs, and evenly sprinkle with the tomatoes and olives.

4. Transfer to the oven and bake until the egg is firm, 14 to 18 minutes. Season with additional salt and pepper to taste (if desired), slice like a pie, and serve warm. Also great as reheated leftovers.

Difficulty: Easy
Prep time: 5 to 10 minutes
Cook time: 20 minutes
   (mostly hands-off)
Makes 4 servings
Special tools: Ovenproof
   10-inch sauté pan

GLUTEN-FREE
DAIRY-FREE
VEGETARIAN
NUT-FREE

1 tablespoon olive oil

½ yellow onion, diced

1 teaspoon paprika

1 teaspoon ground turmeric

¼ teaspoon salt, or more to taste

Ground black pepper

8 eggs, whisked until smooth

2 small Roma (plum) tomatoes (about ¼ pound each), diced

12 pitted black or kalamata olives, sliced (or diced)

SHOPPING LIST

1 small onion	$0.56
1 dozen eggs	$1.19
2 small Roma (plum) tomatoes (about ½ pound)	$1.00
One 3.8-ounce can (or jar) black olives	$1.59
TOTAL	**$4.34**
COST PER SERVING	**$1.09**

PANTRY AND FRIDGE CHECKLIST

1 tablespoon olive oil
1 teaspoon paprika
1 teaspoon ground turmeric
Salt and pepper

INGREDIENTS LEFT OVER

Onion
Eggs
Olives

LISA'S TIP: One recipe tester said this dish was delicious over the Cumin Cheese Toast on page 144!

Cinnamon Roll Pancakes

Difficulty: Easy
Prep time: 10 to 15 minutes
Cook time: 10 to 15 minutes
Makes 4 servings

VEGETARIAN
FREEZER-FRIENDLY

PANCAKES

2 cups whole wheat pastry or
regular whole wheat flour

3 tablespoons ground cinnamon

1 teaspoon baking powder

½ teaspoon salt

1½ cups milk

2 eggs, whisked until smooth

¼ cup pure maple syrup

4 tablespoons (½ stick) butter,
melted, plus more for frying

FROSTING

4 ounces cream cheese, at room
temperature

¼ cup pure maple syrup

2 tablespoons butter, at room
temperature

1 teaspoon pure vanilla extract

Suggested accompaniment:
Fresh fruit

No special occasion needed for these cinnamon roll–inspired pancakes. They're so easy to make that you don't have to wait for the holiday season to enjoy these delicious flavors.

1. If using an electric griddle, preheat it to 350°F.

2. To make the pancakes: In a large bowl, whisk together the flour, cinnamon, baking powder, and salt.

3. Make a well (hole) in the center of the flour mixture and add the milk, eggs, syrup, and melted butter. Whisk until just combined; do not overmix.

4. Coat the griddle or a large skillet placed over medium heat with butter. Using a soup ladle, place one small scoop of batter per pancake on the pan. The batter will be on the thinner side, but will puff up a little during cooking. After a couple minutes, when the pancakes have begun to brown on the bottom, flip and cook the other side until golden. Transfer the pancakes to a plate and repeat to make the rest of the pancakes.

5. To make the frosting: In a bowl, with a hand mixer beat the cream cheese to soften, then beat in the syrup, butter, and vanilla until smooth.

6. Spread the frosting over the pancakes and serve warm with fresh fruit.

SHOPPING LIST

One 3-pound bag whole wheat pastry flour	$3.69
1 pint milk	$0.99
Half dozen eggs	$0.85
8-ounce bottle pure maple syrup	$4.99
One 8-ounce block cream cheese	$2.00
One 8-ounce box butter (2 sticks)	$2.69
TOTAL	**$15.21**
COST PER SERVING	**$3.80**

PANTRY AND FRIDGE CHECKLIST

1 teaspoon pure vanilla extract
3 tablespoons ground cinnamon
1 teaspoon baking powder
Salt

INGREDIENTS LEFT OVER

Flour
Milk
Eggs
Maple syrup
Cream cheese
Butter

Huevos Rancheros (with Shortcut "Refried" Beans)

We were lucky enough to celebrate my husband's cousin's fortieth birthday in Mexico, with friends and family from afar. It's always fun when you get invited to do cool things that you might not do otherwise for milestone birthdays! We not only had a blast, but enjoyed lots of tasty food while we were there, too, including huevos rancheros for breakfast every single morning. So of course I had to re-create my own version once we got home.

Difficulty: Medium
Prep time: 15 minutes
Cook time: 10 to 15 minutes
Makes 4 servings

GLUTEN-FREE
VEGETARIAN
NUT-FREE

SALSA

2 tomatoes, cut into medium dice

1 bell pepper (any color), diced

1 jalapeño pepper, seeded and minced (optional)

1 onion, diced

⅔ cup water

Juice of 1 lime

Salt and ground black pepper

SHORTCUT "REFRIED" BEANS

Two 15.5-ounce cans pinto beans, drained and rinsed

2 cups water

¼ teaspoon ground cumin

¼ teaspoon salt

Ground black pepper

EGGS

1 tablespoon butter

8 eggs

Salt and ground black pepper

FOR SERVING

4 corn tortillas

Grated Monterey Jack or crumbled queso fresco cheese

Cilantro

1. To make the salsa: In a medium saucepan, combine the tomatoes, bell pepper, jalapeño, onion, lime juice, water, and salt and black pepper to taste. Bring to a boil over medium-high heat, then reduce the heat to medium-low and simmer for 10 to 15 minutes. Add more water as needed if the mixture gets too thick.

2. Meanwhile, to make the "refried" beans: In a large skillet, combine the beans, water, cumin, salt, and pepper to taste and bring to a light boil over medium heat. Let it simmer for 3 to 4 minutes, then mash the beans into a paste with a potato masher. Add splashes of water as needed to keep the beans from drying out.

3. To make the eggs: Heat another skillet (or clean the one you made the beans in if you've transferred them to a serving dish) over medium-low heat and melt the butter. Crack the eggs into the pan and cook until done to your liking (I like mine just a touch runny in the middle). Season with salt and pepper.

4. To serve, place a tortilla on each of 4 plates and top with 2 eggs. Spread beans on each plate next to the tortilla. Sprinkle the salsa, cheese, and cilantro on top and serve warm.

(continues on next page)

SHOPPING LIST

2 tomatoes	$3.56
1 bell pepper	$0.99
1 small onion	$0.56
1 lime	$0.25
1 jalapeño pepper	$0.31
Two 15.5-ounce cans pinto beans	$1.82
1 dozen eggs	$1.19
One 8-ounce block Monterey Jack cheese	$3.89
One 8-ounce pack whole-grain corn tortillas	$1.89
TOTAL	**$14.46**
COST PER SERVING	**$3.62**

PANTRY AND FRIDGE CHECKLIST

¼ teaspoon ground cumin
1 tablespoon butter
Salt and pepper
Cilantro (garden)

INGREDIENTS LEFT OVER

Eggs
Monterey Jack cheese

Raspberry Delight Breakfast Smoothie

Before you decide your picky eater will turn their nose up at spinach in a smoothie, please listen to my story! I offered some of this smoothie to a friend of my daughter who'd refused to try lettuce or leafy greens before. She was a little apprehensive, but after her first sip she quickly figured out it actually tasted good and went on to tell me it was "the best smoothie she'd ever had!" After she finished her second helping (thank you very much!), I informed her that spinach was the secret ingredient, which was met with a look of surprise. I'm only okay with "hiding" secret ingredients if you tell your picky eaters about one afterward so they know that particular vegetable or other food isn't so bad after all. Her mom was pleased; I hope this trick works on your little ones as well.

Blend the ingredients together until smooth. Serve cold.

Difficulty: Super easy
Prep time: 5 to 10 minutes
Cook time: N/A
Makes 2 servings
Special tools: Blender

GLUTEN-FREE
VEGETARIAN
NUT-FREE
FREEZER-FRIENDLY

2 bananas, the riper they are the sweeter they'll be (and better, in my opinion)

1 cup fresh spinach

1 cup coconut water or regular water

1 cup frozen raspberries

½ cup plain yogurt

Handful of ice cubes

SHOPPING LIST		PANTRY AND FRIDGE CHECKLIST
2 bananas	$0.40	N/A
One 5-ounce bag spinach	$2.49	
One 11.3-ounce can coconut water	$0.59	**INGREDIENTS LEFT OVER**
One 10-ounce bag frozen raspberries	$3.55	Spinach
One 5.3-ounce container plain yogurt	$1.00	Coconut water
		Raspberries
TOTAL	**$8.03**	Yogurt
COST PER SERVING	**$4.02**	

Budget Granola

Difficulty: Easy
Prep time: 10 to 15 minutes
Cook time: 1 hour 15 minutes
(hands-off)
Makes 3 pounds / 18 to 20
servings
Special tools: Parchment paper
and large rimmed baking
sheet

GLUTEN-FREE (IF GLUTEN-FREE
OATS ARE USED)
DAIRY-FREE (IF COCONUT OIL
IS USED)
VEGETARIAN
FREEZER-FRIENDLY

3½ cups rolled oats

2 cups sliced or chopped raw
almonds

1 cup raw hulled sunflower
seeds

2 teaspoons ground cinnamon

1½ teaspoons ground ginger

½ teaspoon ground nutmeg

½ teaspoon salt

6 tablespoons butter

½ cup honey

2 teaspoons pure vanilla
extract

Homemade granola is my favorite breakfast and I eat it almost every single morning. Even if I'm headed out of town, I bring a bag of it along with me! Aside from the fact that it's super yummy, I like that it keeps me feeling full much longer than any other breakfast I've tried. And with this slightly modified recipe, using only the least expensive nuts and seeds, you can enjoy this breakfast on a budget, too.

1. Preheat the oven to 250°F. Line a large rimmed baking sheet with parchment paper.

2. In a large bowl, mix together the oats, almonds, sunflower seeds, spices, and salt until well combined.

3. In a small pot over low heat, combine the butter and honey. When the butter is completely melted, stir in the vanilla.

4. Pour the wet ingredients over the dry ingredients and mix thoroughly.

5. Using a rubber spatula, spread the mixture onto the baking sheet so it's evenly distributed. Bake until golden brown, about 1 hour 15 minutes.

6. Let the baked granola cool completely, then crumble it as desired and serve with milk or yogurt. Store the granola in an airtight container at room temperature for up to 2 weeks.

SHOPPING LIST		PANTRY AND FRIDGE CHECKLIST
1 pound rolled oats	$1.79	2 teaspoons ground cinnamon
One 8-ounce bag whole raw almonds (will have to slice or chop)	$5.99	1½ teaspoons ground ginger ½ teaspoon ground nutmeg 2 teaspoons pure vanilla extract
One 6.9-ounce container hulled sunflower seeds, raw	$2.99	Salt
One 8-ounce box butter	$2.69	INGREDIENTS LEFT OVER
One 12-ounce jar honey	$2.50	Rolled oats
TOTAL	**$15.96**	Butter
COST PER SERVING (about ½ cup)	**$0.80**	Honey

Loaded Biscuits

I can't think of anything better to go with some fried eggs and fresh fruit for breakfast in the morning! These biscuits are pretty filling, so I like to cut ours small and freeze the extras.

1. Preheat the oven to 425°F.

2. In a large bowl, whisk together the flour, baking powder, and salt. Toss in the butter pieces and use a pastry cutter (an inexpensive tool that makes this job easy) or fork to break up the butter into pea-size pieces. Stir in the Cheddar and bacon. Use a fork to mix in the milk, then bring the dough together with your hands.

3. On a lightly floured surface, flatten the dough into an even layer about 1 inch thick. Cut out rounds using a 2-inch cutter or the rim of a small drinking glass. Reshape the dough and keep cutting so that no dough is wasted.

4. Place the rounds on an ungreased baking sheet, brush the tops with milk, and bake until they begin to turn golden brown and are cooked all the way through, 12 to 15 minutes. Serve warm.

Difficulty: Easy

Prep time: 15 minutes

Cook time: 12 to 15 minutes (hands-off)

Makes twenty to twenty-four 2-inch biscuits

Special tools: Baking sheet and (helpful, but not required) pastry cutter, small round cookie cutter, and brush

NUT-FREE
FREEZER-FRIENDLY

2½ cups whole wheat flour (pastry or regular)

5 teaspoons baking powder

½ teaspoon salt

1 stick (4 ounces) cold butter, cut into tablespoon-size pieces

1 cup grated Cheddar cheese

5 slices bacon, cooked and chopped

1 cup milk, plus more for the biscuit tops

SHOPPING LIST		TOTAL	$15.45	INGREDIENTS LEFT OVER
One 3-pound bag whole wheat pastry flour	$3.69	**COST PER SERVING** (2 biscuits)	**$1.29**	Flour
One 8-ounce box butter	$2.69			Butter
One 8-ounce block Cheddar cheese	$3.89	**PANTRY AND FRIDGE CHECKLIST**		Bacon
One 8-ounce package bacon	$4.19	5 teaspoons baking powder		Milk
1 pint milk	$0.99	Salt		Cheddar cheese

LISA'S TIP: Since you'll have almost half a pack of bacon left over, you could easily double this recipe and freeze the leftover biscuits for school lunches.

Smoked Salmon Cakes

Difficulty: Medium
Prep time: 10 to 15 minutes
Cook time: Less than 10 minutes
Makes 4 servings

NUT-FREE
FREEZER-FRIENDLY

4 ounces smoked salmon, roughly diced

4 ounces cream cheese, at room temperature

2 eggs

¾ cup whole wheat breadcrumbs

½ teaspoon dried dill

¼ teaspoon salt

¼ teaspoon ground black pepper

Olive oil, for cooking

For serving: 4 fried eggs, cooked the way you like them

People sometimes think of smoked salmon as a lunch or dinner ingredient, but it's fabulous served with eggs for breakfast. This would be a great savory dish to make the next time you have houseguests or are tasked with bringing a dish to a brunch gathering. And if you have any leftovers they're also great the next day served over fresh greens for lunch.

1. In a large bowl, mix the salmon, cream cheese, eggs, breadcrumbs, dill, salt, and pepper with a fork until well combined. Form into eight 2½- to 3-inch cakes with your hands.

2. Pour a thin layer of olive oil into the bottom of a large skillet and heat it over medium-low heat. Add the cakes and cook until golden brown and cooked all the way through, 4 to 5 minutes per side.

3. Top with fried eggs and serve.

SHOPPING LIST		PANTRY AND FRIDGE CHECKLIST
One 4-ounce package smoked salmon	$7.99	½ teaspoon dried dill
One 8-ounce block cream cheese	$2.00	Salt and pepper
Half dozen eggs	$0.85	Olive oil, for cooking
One 15-ounce canister whole wheat breadcrumbs	$2.89	**INGREDIENTS LEFT OVER**
TOTAL	**$13.73**	Cream cheese
COST PER SERVING (2 cakes)	**$3.43**	Breadcrumbs

Zucchini Egg Scramble

There's nothing like starting your day with a good dose of veggies! And with the shredded zucchini in this recipe, it cooks in no time at all. I'd even say it's busy-weekday-morning friendly.

1. Trim the zucchini and shred it with a cheese grater. Use a clean, dry kitchen towel to squeeze out all the water.

2. In a medium bowl, lightly whisk the eggs.

3. In a large skillet, melt ½ tablespoon of the butter over medium-low heat. Add the zucchini and cook, stirring, just until it begins to turn translucent, 1 to 2 minutes.

4. Add the remaining ½ tablespoon butter to the pan, pour in the eggs, and cook while slowly stirring and folding over the eggs until they are no longer runny, a couple of minutes more. Mix in the Cheddar, salt, and pepper to taste and cook just until the cheese is melted. Sprinkle the green onions on top and serve warm.

Difficulty: Super easy
Prep time: 5 to 10 minutes
Cook time: Less than 5 minutes
Makes 4 servings

GLUTEN-FREE
VEGETARIAN
NUT-FREE

1 medium zucchini (about ½ pound)
8 eggs
1 tablespoon butter
½ cup shredded sharp Cheddar cheese
⅛ teaspoon salt
Ground black pepper
1 green onion, white and green parts, thiny sliced

SHOPPING LIST

1 medium zucchini (about ½ pound)	$0.85
1 dozen eggs	$1.19
One 8-ounce block sharp Cheddar cheese	$3.89
1 bunch green onions	$0.89
TOTAL	**$6.82**
COST PER SERVING	**$1.71**

PANTRY AND FRIDGE CHECKLIST

| Salt and pepper | |
| 1 tablespoon butter | $0.85 |

INGREDIENTS LEFT OVER

Eggs
Cheddar cheese
Green onions

LISA'S TIP: If you want to check to make sure an egg hasn't gone bad, simply place it (uncracked) in a glass of water. If it sinks, it's fine; if it floats, it's probably been in the fridge for longer than you'd like to know!

Apple Pie French Toast

Difficulty: Easy
Prep time: 10 minutes
Cook time: 10 minutes
Makes 3 to 4 servings

GLUTEN-FREE (IF GLUTEN-FREE BREAD IS USED)
VEGETARIAN
NUT-FREE
FREEZER-FRIENDLY

TOAST

2 eggs

3 tablespoons milk

¼ teaspoon ground cinnamon

3 or 4 slices good-quality whole wheat bread

2 tablespoons butter

APPLE TOPPING

1 tablespoon butter

1 large apple (any variety), unpeeled or peeled, cored and thinly sliced

½ teaspoon ground cinnamon

Pinch of ground nutmeg

2 tablespoons pure maple syrup

There's nothing like a good ol' mashup of a classic dessert and one of our favorite easy breakfasts, especially when no refined sugar is used, so we can eat it first thing in the morning. This is a great dish for older kids to make all by themselves.

1. If using an electric griddle, preheat it to 375°F.

2. To make the toast: In a shallow bowl, whisk the eggs, milk, and cinnamon. Slice the bread pieces in half (I like cutting them diagonally, for triangles). Dip each piece into the egg mixture until well coated.

3. In a large skillet, heat the butter over medium heat (or on the griddle). Cook the toasts until golden brown, 2 to 3 minutes per side. Transfer to a serving platter.

4. To make the apple topping: In either the same pan or simultaneously in another skillet, melt the butter. Add the apple slices, sprinkle with the cinnamon and nutmeg, and cook, stirring gently but often, for 2 to 3 minutes until they begin to soften. Add the maple syrup and cook until the apples are soft when pierced with a fork, another minute or so.

5. Pour the apple mixture over the French toast and serve warm.

SHOPPING LIST		FRIDGE AND PANTRY CHECKLIST
1 loaf high-quality 100% whole wheat bread	$4.99	3 tablespoons butter
Half dozen eggs	$0.85	¾ teaspoon ground cinnamon
1 pint milk	$0.99	Pinch of ground nutmeg
1 large apple	$0.75	2 tablespoons pure maple syrup
TOTAL	**$7.58**	**INGREDIENTS LEFT OVER**
COST PER SERVING	**$1.89**	Bread
		Eggs
		Milk

packed
lunches

packed lunch recipes

Chicken Burrito Bowls

Difficulty: Easy
Prep time: 20 minutes
Cook time: 8 to 10 minutes
Makes 4 servings

GLUTEN-FREE
DAIRY-FREE (IF CHEESE AND SOUR CREAM ARE OMITTED)
NUT-FREE

4 servings cooked brown rice

Juice of ½ lime

½ cup fresh cilantro, chopped

1 teaspoon + 1 tablespoon olive oil

1 pound boneless, skinless chicken breasts (or thighs), cut into 1-inch chunks

1½ teaspoons dried oregano

½ teaspoon ground cumin

½ teaspoon salt

½ teaspoon ground black pepper

½ onion, diced

1½ cups shredded Monterey Jack cheese

2 tomatoes, cut into medium dice

For serving: Sour cream

The first time I made this recipe, my kids were borderline mad at me that I wouldn't let them eat it right away because I was saving it to test the following day served cold in a lunch box. Oh, what a rough life they both lead! Whether you decide to eat this right away or left over, I hope it's as big a hit at your house. It's definitely one of the cookbook favorites for my family.

1. In a large bowl, combine the rice, lime juice, cilantro, and 1 teaspoon of the olive oil. Evenly distribute it among four lunch boxes (or bowls if serving warm).

2. Wipe out the bowl and toss the chicken pieces with the oregano, cumin, salt, and pepper until well coated.

3. In a large skillet, heat the remaining 1 tablespoon olive oil over medium heat. Add the onion and cook, stirring often, until softened, 2 to 3 minutes. Add the chicken and cook, stirring often, until golden brown and no longer pink on the inside, about 5 minutes.

4. Divide the chicken mixture over the rice, then top with the Monterey Jack, tomatoes, and a scoop of sour cream. Store in the fridge (or serve and eat warm).

LISA'S TIP: I love those ready-to-eat microwavable pouches of brown rice in a pinch!

SHOPPING LIST	
One 16-ounce bag brown rice	$1.00
1 lime	$0.25
1 small onion	$0.56
1 pound boneless, skinless chicken breasts	$3.49
One 8-ounce block Monterey Jack cheese	$3.89
2 tomatoes (½ pound)	$0.89
One 8-ounce container sour cream	$0.99
TOTAL	**$11.07**
COST PER SERVING	**$2.21**

PANTRY AND FRIDGE CHECKLIST

Cilantro (garden)
1 tablespoon + 1 teaspoon olive oil
1½ teaspoons dried oregano
½ teaspoon ground cumin
Salt and pepper

INGREDIENTS LEFT OVER

Brown rice
Lime
Onion
Monterey Jack cheese
Sour cream

Pimiento Mac and Cheese

Difficulty: Medium
Prep time: 10 to 15 minutes
Cook time: 5 to 10 minutes
  (after macaroni is cooked)
Makes 4 or 5 servings

VEGETARIAN
NUT-FREE
FREEZER-FRIENDLY

2 tablespoons butter

2 garlic cloves, minced

2 tablespoons whole wheat flour

¾ cup milk

1¼ cups shredded Cheddar cheese

4 tablespoons (2 ounces) cream cheese

¼ cup diced pimientos, with juice

1 teaspoon yellow mustard

½ teaspoon paprika

½ teaspoon salt

1 to 2 drops hot sauce

Ground black or cayenne pepper

2 cups cooked whole wheat elbow macaroni

My younger daughter is a big fan of both macaroni and pimiento cheese, so why not combine the two to switch things up? Sometimes just the slightest adjustments can make a dish you've had a thousand times a new favorite.

1. In a large saucepan, melt the butter over medium-low heat. Add the garlic and cook for just a minute (don't let it burn).

2. Sprinkle the flour over the garlic and whisk until the mixture begins to brown, another minute or two. Whisk in the milk and cook, stirring, until the mixture begins to simmer. Reduce to a light simmer and cook until the mixture thickens, whisking occasionally, another minute or two.

3. Remove from the heat and whisk in the Cheddar, cream cheese, pimientos, mustard, paprika, salt, hot sauce, and black or cayenne pepper to taste. Pour over the macaroni and stir to combine. Refrigerate for 3 or 4 days. (Or serve warm.)

SHOPPING LIST		PANTRY AND FRIDGE CHECKLIST
One 16-ounce box whole wheat elbow macaroni	$0.91	2 tablespoons butter
1 garlic head	$0.50	2 tablespoons whole wheat flour
1 pint milk	$0.99	1 teaspoon mustard
One 8-ounce bag shredded Cheddar cheese	$3.89	½ teaspoon paprika
One 8-ounce block cream cheese	$2.00	Salt
One 4-ounce jar diced pimientos	$1.79	Hot sauce
		Ground black or cayenne pepper
TOTAL	**$10.08**	**INGREDIENTS LEFT OVER**
COST PER SERVING	**$2.02**	Macaroni
		Garlic
		Milk
		Cheddar cheese
		Cream cheese
		Pimientos

"My ten-year-old nephew is not a big eater; he would rather grab a snack than sit for a meal. He generally doesn't like whole wheat pasta or homemade mac and cheese and never likes peppers, mustard, or hot sauce. He started eating the cheese sauce out of the pan with a spoon and then ate a ridiculous-size portion of the finished product for dinner and asked to have the leftovers saved for his lunch tomorrow. He's already asked when I will make it again for him."

—Kim Robert, recipe tester

LISA'S TIP: Jarred pimientos are easy to find here in the South, but I'm told in other regions they are sometimes in the International (Spanish) section, so be sure to ask if you can't find them right away. Worth the effort!

Lemon Poppy Seed Muffins with Toasted Coconut

Difficulty: Easy
Prep time: 15 minutes
Cook time: 18 to 20 minutes
   (hands-off)
Makes 15 muffins
Special tools: Muffin tin and
   liners

VEGETARIAN
NUT-FREE
FREEZER-FRIENDLY

1½ cups whole wheat flour
(regular or pastry)
2 teaspoons grated lemon zest
1 tablespoon poppy seeds
1 teaspoon baking soda
½ teaspoon salt
1 cup plain yogurt
½ cup honey
6 tablespoons butter, melted
2 eggs, whisked
½ cup unsweetened coconut
flakes

"The toasted coconut on
top of these muffins is
my favorite part!"

—Sydney, age 13

We're big fans of muffins at our house. My kids will gobble them up for breakfast, snack, and even lunch. I love to make a big batch and freeze half of them so I can pull one out whenever I need a little lunch-packing help.

1. Preheat the oven to 350°F. Line a muffin tin with liners.

2. In a large bowl, whisk together the flour, lemon zest, poppy seeds, baking soda, and salt.

3. Make a well (hole) in the center of the flour mixture and add the yogurt, honey, melted butter, and eggs. Stir to combine; do not overmix. Use a small ice cream scooper to fill the muffin liners two-thirds to three-quarters full.

4. Evenly sprinkle the coconut flakes over the batter and bake in batches until the coconut just begins to turn golden brown and a toothpick inserted into a muffin comes out clean, 18 to 20 minutes.

SHOPPING LIST		PANTRY AND FRIDGE CHECKLIST
One 2-pound bag whole wheat flour	$3.49	1 tablespoon poppy seeds
1 lemon	$0.65	1 teaspoon baking soda
Two 5.3-ounce containers plain yogurt	$2.00	Salt
One 12-ounce jar honey	$2.50	**INGREDIENTS LEFT OVER**
One 8-ounce box butter	$2.69	Whole wheat flour
Half dozen eggs	$0.85	Lemon
One 7-ounce bag coconut flakes	$2.49	Honey
		Butter
TOTAL	**$14.67**	Eggs
COST PER MUFFIN	**$0.98**	Coconut flakes

Creamy Pasta Salad with Broccoli and Raisins

My younger daughter loves—and I mean loves—this pasta salad! I do think shaving the broccoli thin and mixing it together with kid-friendly macaroni helps make this dish a win-win for the lunch box. And I don't know about you, but I always feel good when I'm able to send veggies to school they'll actually eat.

1. Remove the thick stems from the broccoli and discard (or save to use in another meal). Roughly chop the florets into pieces small enough to fit into the feed tube of a food processor fitted with the thinnest slicing disk and feed the broccoli through. (Or shred into small bite-size pieces by thinly slicing by hand with a knife.) In a large bowl, combine the broccoli, macaroni, raisins, and green onion.

2. In a small bowl, whisk the sour cream, vinegar, honey, mustard, and salt. Pour over the macaroni mixture and stir until well combined. Store in the fridge for up to 5 days. (Or serve right away.)

Difficulty: Easy
Prep time: 15 minutes
Cook time: N/A (after macaroni is cooked)
Makes 4 or 5 servings
Special tools: Food processor with slicing disk (not necessary, but helpful)

GLUTEN-FREE (IF GLUTEN-FREE MACARONI IS USED)
VEGETARIAN
NUT-FREE

½ pound broccoli (about 1 small head)

1½ cups cooked whole wheat elbow macaroni

⅓ cup raisins

1 green onion, white and green parts, thinly sliced

⅔ cup sour cream

1 tablespoon + 1 teaspoon apple cider vinegar

1 tablespoon honey

1 teaspoon yellow mustard

½ teaspoon salt

SHOPPING LIST

One 16-ounce box whole wheat elbow macaroni	$1.69
½ pound broccoli	$1.25
One 12-ounce box raisins	$2.49
1 bunch green onions	$0.89
One 8-ounce container sour cream	$0.99
TOTAL	**$7.31**
COST PER SERVING	**$1.46**

PANTRY AND FRIDGE CHECKLIST
1 tablespoon plus 1 teaspoon apple cider vinegar
1 tablespoon honey
1 teaspoon yellow mustard
Salt

INGREDIENTS LEFT OVER
Elbow macaroni
Raisins
Green onions
Sour cream

"I love creamy sauces, so this is one of my favorite recipes!"

—Sienna, age 11

Classic Potato Salad (Without Mayo!)

Difficulty: Easy
Prep time: 20 minutes
Cook time: 15 to 20 minutes
Makes 6 servings

GLUTEN-FREE
VEGETARIAN
NUT-FREE

2 pounds red potatoes, unpeeled, cut into 1½- to 2-inch chunks

3 eggs

2 celery stalks, finely diced

¼ cup finely diced red onion

2 tablespoons chopped fresh flat-leaf parsley

½ cup sour cream

1 tablespoon yellow mustard

1 tablespoon red wine vinegar

½ teaspoon salt

¼ teaspoon paprika

Ground black pepper

I was on a quest to replace mayonnaise in this classic recipe. As I've explained before, store-bought mayo isn't exactly real food (with five or fewer whole ingredients) and making mayo from scratch isn't really my cup of tea. Plus not everyone is a mayonnaise lover. But now it's no longer an issue with this recipe, which is just as good as the original!

1. Bring a medium pot of water to a boil over high heat. Add the potato chunks and eggs (in the shell) and simmer for 15 minutes. If after 15 minutes the potatoes are not tender when pierced with a fork, remove the eggs and continue boiling the potatoes a few minutes more, until they're done. Drain the potatoes and eggs and run cool water over them.

2. In a large bowl, combine the celery, onion, and parsley. In a small bowl, whisk the sour cream, mustard, red wine vinegar, salt, paprika, and pepper to taste.

3. Cut the potatoes into ½-inch pieces and add them to the large bowl. Peel and dice the eggs (I use a wire egg slicer to cut the egg lengthwise and then crosswise for a quick dice) and add them to the large bowl. Pour the sour cream mixture in and toss to combine. Refrigerate for up to 5 days. (Or serve immediately.)

SHOPPING LIST

2 pounds red potatoes	$2.58
Half dozen eggs	$0.85
1 bunch celery	$2.39
1 small red onion	$0.50
One 8-ounce container sour cream	$0.99
TOTAL	**$7.31**
COST PER SERVING	**$1.22**

PANTRY AND FRIDGE CHECKLIST

Parsley (garden)
1 tablespoon yellow mustard
1 tablespoon red wine vinegar
¼ teaspoon paprika
Salt and pepper

INGREDIENTS LEFT OVER

Eggs
Celery
Onion
Sour cream

Simple Zucchini Soup

Difficulty: Easy
Prep time: 10 minutes
Cook time: 40 minutes (mostly hands-off)
Makes 4 or 5 servings
Special tools: Large rimmed baking sheet and blender (immersion blender or stand blender)

GLUTEN-FREE
DAIRY-FREE (IF PARMESAN CHEESE TOPPING IS OMITTED)
VEGETARIAN (IF VEGETABLE BROTH IS USED)
NUT-FREE
FREEZER-FRIENDLY

3 pounds zucchini (about 6 medium), trimmed and cut into 1-inch dice

3 garlic cloves, smashed

2 tablespoons olive oil

¾ teaspoon dried oregano

¾ teaspoon salt, plus more to taste

Ground black pepper

5 cups veggie or chicken broth (see Tip)

For serving: Freshly grated Parmesan cheese

On a family trip to Italy we had the most amazing zucchini soup I could have ever imagined. I asked the waitress what was in it and she said, "Only zucchini from our garden and broth." My husband and I both said, "That's all?" But sure enough, when we came home it didn't take much for me to re-create this creamy goodness that reminded us of our travels.

1. Preheat the oven to 425°F.

2. On a large rimmed baking sheet, toss together the zucchini, garlic, olive oil, oregano, salt, and pepper to taste. Roast until the zucchini begins to turn translucent and can easily be pierced with a fork, 25 to 30 minutes.

3. Use a silicone spatula to scrape the zucchini and all its spices into a large soup pot. Add the broth and puree until smooth. An immersion hand blender right in the pot makes this an easy job with minimal cleanup. (Otherwise, you'll need to transfer the zucchini and broth to a stand blender and puree, then return it to the soup pot.)

4. Bring to a boil, reduce the heat to low, and simmer for 10 minutes so the flavors can come together.

5. If serving right away, ladle into bowls, season with more salt and pepper (if desired), and generously garnish with Parmesan (you know they did that in Italy!). Or store individual servings for lunches for 4 to 5 days in the refrigerator. Or freeze: I like to use freezer-safe jars for this purpose. Then simply defrost in the fridge the night before school, reheat in the morning, and transfer to an insulated Thermos.

"My six-year-old daughter loves soup but does not like zucchini. She ate three bowls of this and when I told her what it was, she said, 'But I don't like zucchini! I think I must only love zucchini when it's in a soup!'"

—Robin Jenkins, recipe tester

SHOPPING LIST

3 pounds zucchini (about 6
  medium) $5.07
1 garlic head $0.50
One 32-ounce box veggie
  or chicken broth   . $2.09
One 14.5-ounce can veggie
  or chicken broth $1.37
One 6-ounce tub freshly
  grated Parmesan cheease $3.99

TOTAL   **$13.02**
COST PER SERVING   **$2.60**

**PANTRY AND FRIDGE
CHECKLIST**

2 tablespoons olive oil
¾ teaspoon dried oregano
Salt and pepper

INGREDIENTS LEFT OVER
Garlic
Broth (if using store bought)

LISA'S TIP: While you can, of course, use store-bought broth in this recipe, I highly recommend home-made (page 233). I tested it both ways and not only did my family think it was hands-down worth the effort to make homemade, but it'll cost less as well. I guarantee the restaurant in Italy uses homemade broth for their soup, which is part of what made it so amazing. Hard to beat fresh!

Southwest Salad

Difficulty: Easy
Prep time: 15 minutes
Cook time: N/A
Makes 5 or 6 servings
**Special tools: Small jar with
   tight-fitting lid**

GLUTEN-FREE
**DAIRY-FREE (UNLESS RANCH IS
   USED)**
VEGETARIAN
NUT-FREE

SALAD

1 head romaine lettuce, chopped

2 ears corn, boiled for 7 to
8 minutes, then cut off the cob

One 15-ounce can black beans,
drained and rinsed

1 large tomato, diced

CITRUS VINAIGRETTE

3 tablespoons olive oil

2 tablespoons fresh lime juice

1 tablespoon honey

½ teaspoon salt

This salad is perfect to enjoy at the peak of summer with fresh corn and tomatoes. Thanks to the fresh ingredients, it has enough flavor to pair well with the budget-friendly citrus vinaigrette below, but if you really feel like spoiling yourself, try it with creamy Southwest Ranch Dressing (page 255) instead.

1. To make the salad: In a large bowl, toss together the lettuce, corn, black beans, and tomato.

2. To make the citrus vinaigrette: In a jar with a tight-fitting lid, combine the olive oil, lime juice, honey, and salt and shake to emulsify. If serving right away, pour the dressing on top; otherwise store the dressing separately from the salad and re-emulsify the dressing as needed before using.

SHOPPING LIST		PANTRY AND FRIDGE CHECKLIST
1 head romaine lettuce	$2.29	3 tablespoons olive oil
2 ears corn	$1.20	1 tablespoon honey
One 15-ounce can		Salt
black beans	$0.95	
1 large tomato	$0.89	**INGREDIENTS LEFT OVER**
1 lime	$0.50	N/A
TOTAL*	**$5.83**	
COST PER SERVING*	**$0.97**	

*If you choose to splurge by using the Creamy Ranch Dressing, the total is $11.34 and the per-serving cost is $1.89. See page 255 for the Shopping List.

Deconstructed Spring Roll Bowls

Difficulty: Easy
Prep time: 20 minutes
Cook time: N/A (after noodles are cooked)
Makes 4 or 5 servings

GLUTEN-FREE (IF GLUTEN-FREE SOY SAUCE IS USED)
DAIRY-FREE
VEGETARIAN (IF OPTIONAL SHRIMP IS OMITTED)

8 ounces cooked brown rice noodles, Asian style (I like Annie Chun's thin vermicelli-style Maifun noodles)

¼ cup soy sauce

¼ cup peanut butter

1 garlic clove, minced

1 teaspoon toasted sesame oil

1 teaspoon rice vinegar

1 mango, peeled and cut into ½-inch dice

1 cucumber, trimmed and finely diced

⅔ cup salted roasted peanuts

½ cup fresh cilantro, chopped

½ cup fresh mint leaves, chopped

Suggested accompaniment:
1 pound cooked shrimp, cut into medium dice (optional)

Spring rolls with fresh veggies wrapped in rice paper are a fun and tasty kitchen project, but not something we always have time to make. So I'm in love with this just as yummy yet easier "deconstructed" version that would be a welcome sight in my packed lunch any day!

1. Put the noodles in a large bowl.

2. In a small bowl, whisk together the soy sauce, peanut butter, garlic, sesame oil, and vinegar. Toss with the noodles until well combined.

3. Divide the noodle mixture among lunch containers, then top with the mango, cucumber, peanuts, cilantro, mint, and shrimp (if using). If you prefer to keep the peanuts crunchy, store them separately for a packed lunch.

SHOPPING LIST		PANTRY AND FRIDGE CHECKLIST
One 8-ounce box brown rice noodles, Asian style	$4.29	¼ cup soy sauce
One 16-ounce jar peanut butter	$2.67	1 teaspoon toasted sesame oil
1 mango	$1.66	1 teaspoon rice vinegar
1 cucumber	$0.50	Cilantro (garden)
1 garlic head	$0.50	Mint (garden)
One 16-ounce canister salted roasted peanuts	$3.49	**INGREDIENTS LEFT OVER**
TOTAL	**$13.11**	Peanut butter
COST PER SERVING	**$2.62**	Garlic
		Peanuts

LISA'S TIP: If you choose to use shrimp in this recipe, I've got some advice to share. I prefer to buy shrimp from my continent and already deveined (and if possible, shelled as well). When I'm lucky enough to find shrimp like this, I always ask if the store has an extra bag in the back that's still frozen. It doesn't take long to thaw frozen shrimp in a bowl of cool water, so it's wonderful to have on hand in the freezer for whenever I need it.

It also takes only a few minutes to cook shrimp for this (or any other) recipe. You can either boil it in a pot of water or pat it dry and sear it in a skillet with some butter over medium heat until it's pink and firm all the way through.

Portobello Tartine

Difficulty: Super easy
Prep time: 10 minutes
Cook time: 5 minutes
Makes 2 servings
Special tools: Small jar with tight-fitting lid

GLUTEN-FREE (IF GLUTEN-FREE BREAD IS USED)
VEGETARIAN
NUT-FREE

2 tablespoons olive oil

1 tablespoon balsamic vinegar

1 tablespoon chopped fresh basil

1 garlic clove, minced

Salt and ground black pepper

2 small to medium portobello caps, cut into ¼-inch-wide slices

2 to 3 slices whole wheat sandwich bread (depending on size)

2 to 3 slices provolone cheese

2 tablespoons butter

Family members of mine who aren't even big mushroom fans love this tartine, which is basically just an open-faced sandwich, so give it a shot! I would eat this cold in my lunch box over a tired old deli meat sandwich any day.

1. In a small jar with a tight-fitting lid, combine the oil, vinegar, basil, garlic, and salt and pepper to taste. Shake to emulsify.

2. Place the mushroom slices in a small bowl, drizzle the olive oil mixture on top, and toss to combine. Evenly distribute the mushrooms on the slices of bread and top each one with a slice of provolone.

3. In a medium sauté pan with a tight-fitting lid, heat the butter over medium-low heat. Place the tartines bread side down in the pan. Cook until the bread just begins to turn golden brown on the bottom, 3 to 5 minutes. Cover with the lid, remove from the heat, and let sit until the cheese melts but the bread does not burn, a couple minutes more. Eat warm or cold within 24 hours.

SHOPPING LIST	
1 head garlic	$0.50
One 6-ounce package portobello caps	$3.69
1 loaf good-quality whole wheat bread	$4.99
One 8-ounce pack sliced provolone cheese	$3.39
TOTAL	**$12.57**
COST PER SERVING	**$6.29**

PANTRY AND FRIDGE CHECKLIST

2 tablespoons olive oil
1 tablespoon balsamic vinegar
Basil (garden)
2 tablespoons butter
Salt and pepper

INGREDIENTS LEFT OVER

Garlic
Bread
Provolone cheese

Easy Chickpea Salad

Whether you eat this by itself as a side dish or spoon it over some lettuce as a main dish, you'll love how fresh-tasting and portable this recipe is. Make a big batch on Sunday and you'll have it to enjoy all week long.

1. In a large bowl, toss together the chickpeas, cucumber, bell pepper, and onion.

2. In a small jar with a tight-fitting lid, combine the olive oil, vinegar, garlic, and basil. Shake to emulsify.

3. Pour the dressing over the chickpea mixture, season with salt and pepper to taste, and toss to combine. Eat or store in the fridge for up to 5 days.

Difficulty: Super easy
Prep time: 15 minutes
Cook time: N/A
Makes 6 side servings
Special tools: Small jar with tight-fitting lid

GLUTEN-FREE
DAIRY-FREE
VEGETARIAN
NUT-FREE

One 15-ounce can chickpeas, drained and rinsed
1 cucumber, finely diced
1 red bell pepper, finely diced
½ red onion, finely diced
3 tablespoons olive oil
2 tablespoons red wine vinegar
2 garlic cloves, minced
½ cup fresh basil leaves, chopped
Salt and ground black pepper

SHOPPING LIST

One 15-ounce can chickpeas	$0.91
1 cucumber	$0.50
1 red bell pepper	$2.19
1 red onion	$0.75
1 garlic head	$0.50
TOTAL	**$4.85**
COST PER SERVING	**$0.81**

PANTRY AND FRIDGE CHECKLIST

3 tablespoons olive oil
2 tablespoons red wine vinegar
Basil leaves (garden)
Salt and pepper

INGREDIENTS LEFT OVER

Red onion
Garlic

Creamy Kale Caesar Salad

Difficulty: Super easy
Prep time: 10 to 15 minutes
Cook time: N/A
Makes 4 servings

GLUTEN-FREE
VEGETARIAN

1 large bunch kale, any variety
(could also use spinach)

⅓ cup chopped walnuts, lightly
toasted (see Tip)

¼ cup sour cream

¼ cup freshly grated
Parmesan cheese

3 tablespoons olive oil

1 tablespoon fresh lemon juice

1 garlic clove, minced

¼ teaspoon salt

Ground black pepper

My kids love anything creamy—so much so that they'll even overlook the kale in this dish. And this happens to be my favorite kale salad, so it's a win-win when this is on the menu at our house.

1. Remove and discard the large stems and center ribs from the kale and cut the leaves into narrow strips. Toss in a large bowl with the toasted walnuts.

2. In a smaller bowl, whisk the sour cream, Parmesan, olive oil, lemon juice, garlic, and salt and pepper to taste. Pour the dressing over the kale mixture, toss to coat, and eat within 24 hours.

SHOPPING LIST		PANTRY AND FRIDGE CHECKLIST
1 bunch kale	$1.99	3 tablespoons olive oil
One 6-ounce bag raw walnuts	$3.29	Salt and pepper
One 8-ounce container sour cream	$0.99	**INGREDIENTS LEFT OVER**
One 6-ounce tub freshly grated Parmesan cheese	$3.99	Walnuts
1 lemon	$0.65	Sour cream
1 garlic head	$0.50	Parmesan cheese
		Garlic
TOTAL	**$11.61**	
COST PER SERVING	**$2.90**	

LISA'S TIP: I like to toast raw nuts and seeds in a dry skillet over medium-low heat or in a toaster oven while stirring frequently. Either way, it's important to keep a close eye on them because they can go from browned to burned very quickly!

Smoked Salmon Wraps

Our first backpacking trip with the kids was a guided tour in Banff, Canada, with a company that not only provided all the equipment (we did fly there, after all), but prepared all our food. It was the perfect way to get our feet wet with taking the children on this type of adventure, and to this day I'll never forget the first lunch they had for us out in the wilderness: smoked salmon wraps. I've always been a smoked salmon fan but never thought to have it in a wrap before that trip, so I'm excited to share this version, which we now love to make at home.

1. In a medium bowl, mix the cream cheese, pimientos, garlic, paprika, and hot sauce until smooth.

2. Spread the cream cheese mixture over the tortillas or wraps. Top with salmon and cucumber, then roll up and eat within 1 to 2 days.

Difficulty: Easy
Prep time: 15 minutes
Cook time: N/A
Makes 4 or 5 servings

GLUTEN-FREE (IF GLUTEN-FREE WRAPS ARE USED)
NUT-FREE

4 ounces cream cheese, at room temperature

3 tablespoons diced jarred pimientos, with juice

1 garlic clove, minced

¼ teaspoon paprika

3 to 4 drops hot sauce (I use Tabasco)

4 or 5 large whole wheat tortillas/wraps

4 ounces smoked salmon

1 cucumber, trimmed, seeded, and cut into thin strips

SHOPPING LIST	
One 8-ounce package cream cheese	$2.00
One 4-ounce jar diced pimientos with juice	$1.79
1 garlic head	$0.50
One 10-count package whole wheat tortillas	$2.35
One 4-ounce package smoked salmon	$7.99
1 cucumber	$0.50
TOTAL	**$15.13**
COST PER SERVING	**$3.03**

PANTRY AND FRIDGE CHECKLIST
¼ teaspoon paprika
Hot sauce

INGREDIENTS LEFT OVER
Cream cheese
Pimientos
Garlic
Tortillas

CHAPTER 4

salads
and sides

salad and side recipes

My Favorite Summer Salad

One of my favorite parts of summer is all the fresh, locally grown tomatoes. If you think you don't like tomatoes and you've only had them from the grocery store, then that's the reason. The homegrown version tastes almost like a completely different vegetable altogether, so delicious and sweet compared to the flavorless mass-market ones. Trust me on this!

1. To make the salad: In a large bowl, toss together the lettuce, peach, tomato, mozzarella, onion, basil, and salt and pepper to taste.

2. To make the dressing: In a small jar with a tight-fitting lid, combine the olive oil and vinegar and shake to emulsify. Toss with the salad and serve.

SHOPPING LIST		PANTRY AND FRIDGE CHECKLIST
1 head Bibb lettuce	$2.49	Basil (garden)
1 peach or nectarine	$1.25	2 tablespoons olive oil
1 tomato	$0.89	2 teaspoons balsamic vinegar
One 8-ounce package fresh mozzarella	$6.99	Salt and pepper
1 red onion	$0.75	**INGREDIENTS LEFT OVER**
TOTAL	**$12.37**	Mozzarella
COST PER SERVING	**$2.06**	Red onion

Difficulty: Super easy
Prep time: 15 to 20 minutes
Cook time: N/A
Makes 5 or 6 servings
Special tools: Small jar with tight-fitting lid

GLUTEN-FREE
VEGETARIAN
NUT-FREE

SALAD

1 head Bibb lettuce, chopped

1 peach or nectarine, diced

1 tomato, cut into ½-inch dice

6 ounces fresh mozzarella cheese, cut into ½-inch dice

¼ red onion, thinly sliced

¼ cup fresh basil leaves, chopped or thinly sliced

Salt and ground black pepper

DRESSING

2 tablespoons olive oil

2 teaspoons balsamic vinegar

Rainbow Salad with Salmon

Difficulty: Easy
Prep time: 15 to 20 minutes
Cook time: 12 to 15 minutes
(hands-off)
Makes 4 servings
Special tools: Loaf pan

DAIRY-FREE
**GLUTEN-FREE (IF GLUTEN-FREE SOY
SAUCE IS USED)**
NUT-FREE

¾ pound skinned salmon fillets
Asian Salad Dressing (page 256)
5 ounces mixed salad greens
1 large mango, peeled, seeded,
and diced
4 radishes, trimmed and thinly
sliced

"My family loved this recipe. I must confess—I'd never tried a radish before tonight, and I'd never cut up a fresh mango. But we all had a good experience; even my pickiest eater tasted everything and liked it. He couldn't believe he ate a radish!"

—Valerie Urnis, recipe tester

This recipe is one of those accidents that turned out to be a good thing. I was trying to create a salmon recipe and it just didn't work out, so I quickly sautéed the salmon instead. At the same time, I was also cutting up a mango for school lunches and happened to be making Asian Salad Dressing, and everything ended up together on our plates, for one accidentally yummy combination!

1. Preheat the oven to 450°F.

2. Place the salmon in a small loaf pan and pour half the dressing on top, along with enough water to just cover the salmon (about ⅓ cup). Bake until light pink all the way through and flaky, 12 to 14 minutes. Cut with a fork into bite-size pieces and set aside in the marinade.

3. Divide the salad greens, mango, and radishes among 4 salad bowls. Top with the salmon and the remaining dressing and serve.

SHOPPING LIST		PANTRY AND FRIDGE CHECKLIST
¾ pound wild-caught salmon fillets	$7.49	N/A
One 5-ounce package mixed salad greens	$2.99	**INGREDIENTS LEFT OVER**
1 mango	$1.66	Radishes
One 16-ounce bag radishes	$1.69	
Asian Salad Dressing (page 256)	$1.13	
TOTAL	**$14.96**	
COST PER SERVING	**$3.74**	

LISA'S TIP: There are lots of ways to cut a mango—here's mine. Make sure the mango is ripe and ready (a little soft—similar to a ripe avocado). Peel the skin off with a carrot peeler. Now you'll use a mango slicer, which makes it really easy. Position the mango upright and slice right down the middle with the mango slicer. Lay the mango pieces flat on a cutting board and dice away, then pick up the seed and nibble off the bits that stayed attached, of course!

Green Apple–Cucumber Slaw

Here's a twist on typical coleslaw that can easily be thrown together any time of year. Even with the little bit of vinegar in this one, my kids were all over this dish. It's a definite crowd pleaser.

1.   In a large bowl, whisk together the sour cream, vinegar, honey, and salt and pepper to taste.

2.   Add the cucumber, apple, and green onion and toss until well combined. Serve or store in the refrigerator for up to 2 days.

Difficulty: Super easy
Prep time: 15 minutes
Cook time: N/A
Makes 6 servings

GLUTEN-FREE
VEGETARIAN
NUT-FREE

¼ cup sour cream

2 tablespoons apple cider vinegar

1 tablespoon honey

Salt and ground black pepper

1 cucumber, trimmed, halved lengthwise, and cut into thin half-moons

2 Granny Smith apples, cored and cut into thin slices

2 green onions, white and green parts, chopped

SHOPPING LIST		PANTRY AND FRIDGE CHECKLIST
1 cucumber	$0.50	2 tablespoons apple cider vinegar
2 Granny Smith apples (1 pound)	$2.29	1 tablespoon honey
1 bunch green onions	$0.89	Salt and pepper
One 8-ounce container sour cream	$0.99	**INGREDIENTS LEFT OVER**
TOTAL	**$4.67**	Green onions
COST PER SERVING	**$0.78**	Sour cream

"Surprisingly tasty! I didn't think I would like sour cream and green onions with apples, but this is a nice combination."

—Mary Rosewood, recipe tester

LISA'S TIP: To make the apple slicing easy in this recipe, I used an apple corer/slicer and then sliced each piece two more times.

Campfire Potatoes

Difficulty: Super easy
Prep time: 5 to 10 minutes
Cook time: 40 to 45 minutes in the oven or 25 to 30 minutes in the campfire
Makes 4 or 5 servings
Special tools: Foil and parchment paper (optional)

GLUTEN-FREE
DAIRY-FREE
VEGETARIAN
NUT-FREE

1½ pounds small (new) potatoes, any color or a mix, sliced in half

2 garlic cloves, minced

1 tablespoon olive oil

½ teaspoon salt

Ground black pepper

The best thing about cooking food in foil packets (other than that they're fun to make) is that there's very little cleanup when you're done. And this recipe is a reminder that you can keep it simple with foil packets whether you have a campfire to cook over or not; veggies or potatoes with seasonings are all it takes to cook this way!

1. Preheat the oven to 450°F or start a campfire.

2. Lay two 18-inch pieces of foil on top of each other, crosswise. Line with parchment paper if desired.

3. Lay the potatoes on top of the foil stack and toss/coat with the garlic, oil, salt, and pepper to taste.

4. Grab the two exposed ends of the bottom piece of foil and fold together. Bring the other two ends together and crimp as well to secure the grill pack.

5. Place in the oven or toss onto the hot coals of the campfire. Roast until the potatoes are tender when pierced with a fork, 40 to 45 minutes in the oven or 25 to 30 minutes in the campfire. You can also use an outdoor grill.

SHOPPING LIST		PANTRY AND FRIDGE CHECKLIST
One 28-ounce bag small (new) potatoes	$4.49	1 tablespoon olive oil
1 garlic head	$0.50	Salt and pepper
TOTAL	**$4.99**	**INGREDIENTS LEFT OVER**
COST PER SERVING	**$1.00**	Potatoes
		Garlic

LISA'S TIP: These potatoes would be great with a little fresh rosemary or thyme mixed in as well!

Black Bean and Sweet Potato Cakes

We love traditional potato cakes (made with white potatoes), so I knew this Mexican-inspired version would be a big hit as well! This is a great veggie side item to go with tacos or burritos and would even make a great topper for a big plate of salad.

1. Shred the sweet potato in the food processor fitted with the shredding disk (or use a cheese grater to shred the potato by hand).

2. In a large bowl, combine the sweet potato, beans, corn, flour, and spices. Stir to combine. Mix in the eggs, then use your hands to form the mixture into 12 thin patties, each about 3 inches wide.

3. In a large skillet, heat a thin layer of olive oil over medium-low heat. Add 6 patties and cook until golden brown on both sides, 3 to 4 minutes per side. Repeat to make the rest of the cakes, adding a little more olive oil if the pan is dry. Top with sour cream and serve.

Difficulty: Medium
Prep time: 15 to 20 minutes (or longer without a food processor)
Cook time: 12 to 16 minutes
Makes about twelve 3-inch cakes
Special tools: Food processor (not necessary, but helpful)

DAIRY-FREE (IF SOUR CREAM IS OMITTED)
VEGETARIAN
NUT-FREE
FREEZER-FRIENDLY

1 medium sweet potato (about 12 ounces), unpeeled
One 15-ounce can black beans, drained and rinsed
½ cup frozen corn kernels
½ cup whole wheat flour
1 tablespoon chili powder
1 teaspoon ground cumin
1 teaspoon salt
2 eggs, whisked
Olive oil, for cooking

For serving: Sour cream

SHOPPING LIST		PANTRY AND FRIDGE CHECKLIST
One medium sweet potato (about 12 ounces)	$0.97	1 tablespoon chili powder
One 15-ounce can black beans	$0.95	1 teaspoon ground cumin
One 15-ounce bag frozen corn kernels	$1.69	Salt
One 2-pound bag whole wheat flour	$3.49	Olive oil, for cooking
Half dozen eggs	$0.85	**INGREDIENTS LEFT OVER**
One 8-ounce container sour cream	$0.99	Frozen corn
TOTAL	**$8.94**	Whole wheat flour
COST PER SERVING (2 cakes)	**$1.49**	Eggs
		Sour cream

Melt-in-Your-Mouth Cream Biscuits

Difficulty: Super easy
Prep time: 10 to 15 minutes
Cook time: 10 to 12 minutes
 (hands-off)
Makes 16 biscuits
Special tools: Large baking sheet

VEGETARIAN
NUT-FREE
FREEZER-FRIENDLY

**2 cups whole wheat pastry
flour, plus more for patting out
the dough**

2½ teaspoons baking powder

½ teaspoon salt

1¼ cups heavy cream

**Milk, for brushing the tops
(optional)**

Suggested accompaniment:
Butter and jam

*I knew this biscuit recipe was a hit when my daughter kept saying, "Why are these
so good?" You've got to love a kitchen win like that! And they're so incredibly easy
to make—even easier than my original biscuit recipe on my blog and in my first
cookbook. Now, if only I could just keep these on hand for more than a few hours,
we'd be in good shape.*

1. Preheat the oven to 450°F.

2. In a large bowl, use a fork to whisk the pastry flour, baking powder, and salt. Pour in the cream and stir to combine just until the dry
ingredients are moistened.

3. Pick up the dough with your hands, set it on a large baking sheet,
and pat it into a big square about ½ inch thick. Use extra flour as
needed to keep it from sticking to your hands.

4. Cut the dough into 16 equal squares, then spread them out on
the baking sheet so they are at least an inch or two apart. Brush the
tops with milk if desired (for browner tops).

5. Bake until the biscuits are golden brown on the bottom, 10 to
12 minutes. Serve warm with butter and jam or store at room temperature in an airtight container for 4 to 5 days.

SHOPPING LIST		PANTRY AND FRIDGE CHECKLIST
One 3-pound bag whole wheat pastry flour	$3.69	2½ teaspoons baking powder
1 pint heavy cream	$3.04	Salt
TOTAL	**$6.73**	**INGREDIENTS LEFT OVER**
COST PER SERVING		Flour
(2 biscuits)	**$0.84**	Heavy cream

Kale and Bacon–Stuffed Potatoes

If you're trying to get more greens into your diet (aren't we all?), then I've got a recipe for you. I already love baked potatoes, but mixing the potatoes with more yummy good stuff and putting it back in? Oh my, even better. My whole family gobbled up these potatoes, and I think they're filling enough to serve as the main dish. They would pair wonderfully with a soup and salad. Enjoy!

1. Preheat the oven to 425°F.

2. Scrub the potatoes clean, prick a few holes in the skin with a fork, and bake on a small baking sheet until tender when pierced with a fork, 45 to 55 minutes. (Or cook the potatoes in the microwave if you are short on time.)

3. Meanwhile, in a large skillet, cook the bacon over medium heat for several minutes, or until the bacon starts to curl up and darken on the bottom. Flip and cook to your desired doneness. I like my bacon crispy, so I cook it until both sides are dark brown. Drain on paper towels and crumble it. Pour all but 1 tablespoon of the bacon grease out of the skillet, reserve it, and set the skillet aside.

4. Wash the kale, cut out and discard the large stems and center ribs, and cut or tear the leaves into shreds (you'll have about 4 cups shredded kale). Heat the bacon grease in the skillet over medium heat and add the kale and garlic. Cook and stir until the kale wilts (adding a tablespoon of water if necessary to help), 1 to 2 minutes.

5. When the potatoes are ready, remove them from the oven. Leave the oven on and increase the temperature to 450°F.

Difficulty: Medium
Prep time: 20 minutes
Cook time: 55 to 70 minutes (mostly hands-off)
Makes 6 potato halves
Special tools: Small baking sheet

GLUTEN-FREE
NUT-FREE
FREEZER-FRIENDLY

3 russet (baking) potatoes (about 2 pounds total)

4 slices bacon (with grease reserved after cooking)

½ bunch lacinato (dinosaur) or curly kale

1 garlic clove, minced

⅔ cup freshly grated Parmesan cheese

½ cup sour cream

¼ cup milk (optional)

2 tablespoons butter

½ teaspoon salt, or more to taste

Ground black pepper

(continues on next page)

6. Slice the potatoes in half lengthwise and carefully scoop the insides into a large bowl (while taking care not to break the outer shell) and gently mash to break up any large chunks. Add the bacon, kale, Parmesan, sour cream, milk (if using), butter, salt, and pepper to taste and stir until well combined. Do not overmix.

7. Scoop the potato mixture back into the potato shells and bake until the tops turn golden brown, 10 to 15 minutes. Sprinkle with salt to taste and serve warm. Store any leftovers in the fridge for up to 5 days (they're great left over!).

SHOPPING LIST

2 pounds russet potatoes	$2.58
One 8-ounce package bacon	$4.19
1 bunch kale	$1.99
One 6-ounce tub freshly grated Parmesan cheese	$3.99
1 garlic head	$0.50
One 8-ounce container sour cream	$0.99
TOTAL	**$14.24**
COST PER SERVING (1 potato half)	**$2.37**

PANTRY AND FRIDGE CHECKLIST

2 tablespoons butter
Salt and pepper

INGREDIENTS LEFT OVER

Bacon
Kale
Parmesan cheese
Garlic
Sour cream

"I made a vegetarian version without bacon for my daughter—still good!"

—Claudia Walter, recipe tester
(Good to know for those who don't eat meat . . . or want to save even more money.)

Shredded Brussels Sprouts

Difficulty: Easy

Prep time: 10 to 15 minutes (longer without a food processor)

Cook time: 6 to 7 minutes

Makes 4 servings

Special tools: Food processor (not necessary, but helpful)

GLUTEN-FREE
DAIRY-FREE (IF PARMESAN IS OMITTED)
VEGETARIAN
NUT-FREE

8 ounces Brussels sprouts, trimmed

2 tablespoons olive oil

1 teaspoon balsamic vinegar

¼ cup freshly grated Parmesan cheese

Ground black pepper

It's amazing how a simple change can reinvent Brussels sprouts! We thankfully already enjoy them, but this recipe switched things up enough to make us love them even more. This would be a lovely addition to any holiday dinner table, but it's easy enough for a busy weeknight as well.

1. Run the Brussels sprouts through the feed tube of a food processor fitted with a slicing disk until all are shredded (or shred them by hand).

2. In a large skillet, heat the olive oil over medium heat and add the sprouts. Cook, stirring occasionally, until tender, 6 to 7 minutes.

3. Remove from heat and mix in the balsamic vinegar, Parmesan, and pepper to taste.

SHOPPING LIST		PANTRY AND FRIDGE CHECKLIST	
One 8-ounce bag Brussels sprouts	$2.79	2 tablespoons olive oil	
One 6-ounce tub freshly grated Parmesan cheese	$3.99	1 teaspoon balsamic vinegar	
		Pepper	
TOTAL	**$6.78**	**INGREDIENTS LEFT OVER**	
COST PER SERVING	**$1.70**	Parmesan cheese	

Zucchini and Feta Fritters

This is a fabulous summer side item to make great use of in-season zucchini and mint. The fritters would pair perfectly with some grilled steaks or chicken and fresh watermelon slices. But don't let cold weather stop you—you can definitely fry these up any time of year.

1. Shred the zucchini using the largest holes on a cheese grater (or a food processor with a shredding disk). Use a clean kitchen towel to squeeze out as much liquid from the zucchini as you can (discard the liquid). Transfer to a large bowl and stir in the eggs, feta, onion, cumin, salt, and pepper to taste. Stir in the flour.

2. In a large skillet, heat a thin layer of olive oil over medium-low heat. Scoop out the zucchini mixture using a ¼-cup measure and drop it into the pan, repeating to make as many patties as will fit in the skillet. Gently flatten the patties with the back of a spatula and cook until golden brown on both sides and cooked all the way through, 3 to 5 minutes per side. Repeat to make the rest of the fritters.

Difficulty: Medium
Prep time: 15 minutes
Cook time: 12 to 15 minutes (if made in two batches)
Makes 14 to 16 fritters

VEGETARIAN
NUT-FREE
FREEZER-FRIENDLY

3 medium zucchini (about 1½ pounds)
2 eggs, whisked
½ cup crumbled feta cheese
¼ cup diced yellow onion
⅓ cup fresh mint leaves, chopped
½ teaspoon ground cumin
½ teaspoon salt
Ground black pepper
1 cup whole wheat flour
Olive oil, for cooking

SHOPPING LIST

3 medium zucchini (about 1½ pounds)	$2.54
Half dozen eggs	$0.85
One 4-ounce tub crumbled feta cheese	$2.49
1 small yellow onion	$0.56
One 2-pound bag whole wheat flour	$3.49
TOTAL	**$9.93**
COST PER SERVING (2 to 3 fritters)	**$1.66**

PANTRY AND FRIDGE CHECKLIST

½ teaspoon ground cumin
Mint (garden)
Salt and pepper
Olive oil, for cooking

INGREDIENTS LEFT OVER

Whole wheat flour
Eggs
Onion

"My twelve-year-old son, who has only ever been willing to eat corn and green beans, ate these fritters and *loved* them! I was so excited that I finally found a way to get him to eat another green vegetable!"

—Shari Ramsey, recipe tester

Sheet Pan Brussels Sprouts and Potatoes

Difficulty: Super easy

Prep time: 10 to 15 minutes

Cook time: 25 to 30 minutes (hands-off)

Makes 6 servings

Special tools: 13 x 18-inch rimmed baking sheet and small jar with tight-fitting lid

GLUTEN-FREE
DAIRY-FREE
VEGETARIAN
NUT-FREE

1½ pounds Brussels sprouts, trimmed and halved

1½ pounds fingerling or new potatoes, halved

4 or 5 garlic cloves, minced

2 tablespoons olive oil

2 teaspoons apple cider vinegar

¾ teaspoon salt

Ground black pepper

One night I was arriving home from out of town right at 5 p.m. on a school night and started brainstorming types of super-easy dinners I could possibly make. I knew it had to be quick or I'd be tempted to eat out (not my first choice after having been away). The winning home-cooked dinner turned out to be Simple Seafood (from my first cookbook—I love how fish takes no time at all to cook) with a side of these Brussels sprouts and potatoes, which I've since made again and again!

1. Preheat the oven to 425°F.

2. Place the sprouts, potatoes, and garlic on a rimmed baking sheet.

3. In a small jar with a tight-fitting lid, shake the oil, vinegar, salt, and pepper to taste until emulsified. Pour over the veggies and toss with your hands until thoroughly coated.

4. Bake until the veggies are golden brown and tender when pierced with a fork, 25 to 30 minutes. Serve warm.

SHOPPING LIST		PANTRY AND FRIDGE CHECKLIST
One 16-ounce bag + an 8-ounce bag Brussels sprouts	$7.28	2 tablespoons olive oil 2 teaspoons apple cider vinegar Salt and pepper
One 28-ounce bag fingerling or new potatoes	$4.49	**INGREDIENTS LEFT OVER**
1 garlic head	$0.50	Potatoes
TOTAL	**$12.27**	
COST PER SERVING	**$2.05**	

Stir-Fry Broccoli

This is officially my new favorite way to eat broccoli! I often fall into a rut of steaming it, which is probably why it isn't my favorite veggie. But it's amazing how much more I like it thinned out like this and sautéed with a little bit of extra flavor. I love to serve it alongside Asian-inspired dishes like the Slow Cooker Mongolian Beef (page 220) or Slow Cooker Moo Shu Shredded Pork (page 229).

1. Remove the big stems from the broccoli and discard. Roughly chop the florets into pieces small enough to fit into the large feed tube of a food processor fitted with the thinnest slicing disk. Feed the broccoli through (or use a knife to thinly shave it into small bite-size pieces).

2. In a wok or cast-iron (or other) skillet, melt the coconut oil over high heat. Cook the broccoli, stirring occasionally, until slightly charred, 3 to 4 minutes.

3. Add the garlic and cook, stirring, for 30 to 60 seconds, taking care not to let it burn. Transfer to a large platter or bowl, season with salt and pepper to taste, and serve.

Difficulty: Super easy
Prep time: 10 to 15 minutes
Cook time: 5 minutes
Makes 4 servings
Special tools: Food processor (not necessary, but helpful)

GLUTEN-FREE
DAIRY-FREE
VEGETARIAN
NUT-FREE

1 pound broccoli
1 tablespoon coconut oil
3 garlic cloves, thinly sliced
Salt and ground black pepper

SHOPPING LIST		PANTRY AND FRIDGE CHECKLIST
1 pound broccoli	$2.50	1 tablespoon coconut oil
1 garlic head	$0.50	Salt and pepper
TOTAL	**$3.00**	
COST PER SERVING	**$0.75**	**INGREDIENTS LEFT OVER**
		Garlic

"I didn't think my kids would like this recipe; we always steam our broccoli and they usually insist on it plain. I put this broccoli in a bowl and turned my back and was shocked to hear *mmms* in the background and somebody saying, 'Make it again, Mom!' My ten-year-old son ate it like popcorn in front of his computer!"

—Chandra Smolen, recipe tester

Coconut Rice

Difficulty: Super easy
Prep time: 5 to 10 minutes
Cook time: 20 to 40 minutes,
   depending on type of rice
Makes 4 servings

GLUTEN-FREE
DAIRY-FREE
VEGETARIAN
FREEZER-FRIENDLY
NUT-FREE

1 cup uncooked brown rice

¾ cup coconut milk (shake the
can before opening, then stir
until smooth)

1 cup water

1 green onion, white and green
parts, sliced

1 teaspoon toasted sesame
seeds, or buy raw and toast
them yourself (see page 100)

¼ teaspoon salt, or more to
taste

Plain brown rice can get a little boring, so this is my new favorite way to make it. This recipe is great paired with Easy Chinese Chicken (page 168) and Maple-Roasted Sweet Potatoes and Carrots (opposite) for a complete, satisfying meal that's easy enough to throw together on a busy weeknight.

1.   In a small saucepan, whisk the rice, coconut milk, and water in a small saucepan and bring to a boil over high heat. Cover, reduce the heat to low, and simmer until the rice is tender, anywhere from 20 to 40 minutes, depending on the type of rice and package directions.

2.   Stir in the green onion, sesame seeds, and salt and serve warm.

SHOPPING LIST		PANTRY AND FRIDGE CHECKLIST
One 16-ounce bag brown rice	$1.00	Salt
One 13.5-ounce can coconut milk	$1.49	**INGREDIENTS LEFT OVER**
1 bunch green onions	$0.89	Brown rice
One 1-ounce container toasted sesame seeds	$3.29	Coconut milk Green onions Sesame seeds
TOTAL	**$6.67**	
COST PER SERVING	**$1.67**	

Maple-Roasted Sweet Potatoes and Carrots

This is one of my favorite new side items. It's perfect for when you could use a break from green veggies and pairs beautifully with the Easy Chinese Chicken (page 168) and Coconut Rice (opposite).

1. Preheat the oven to 400°F.

2. Line a baking sheet with parchment and toss all the ingredients together on the sheet.

3. Bake until tender when pierced with a fork, 25 to 30 minutes, stirring a couple times to ensure even cooking.

Difficulty: Easy
Prep time: 15 to 20 minutes
Cook time: 20 to 25 minutes
   (hands-off)
Makes 3 or 4 side servings
Special tools: Baking sheet and
   parchment paper

GLUTEN-FREE
DAIRY-FREE
VEGETARIAN
NUT-FREE

1 large sweet potato, unpeeled, cut into 1-inch dice

4 carrots, peeled and cut into 1-inch dice

2 tablespoons coconut oil

2 tablespoons pure maple syrup

SHOPPING LIST		PANTRY AND FRIDGE CHECKLIST
1 large sweet potato (about 16 ounces)	$1.29	2 tablespoons coconut oil
1 pound bag carrots	$0.99	2 tablespoons pure maple syrup
TOTAL	**$2.28**	**INGREDIENTS LEFT OVER**
COST PER SERVING	**$0.57**	Carrots

Cheesy Mashed Potato Casserole

Difficulty: Easy
Prep time: 15 minutes
Cook time: 26 to 28 minutes
Makes 6 servings
Special tools: Potato masher or electric mixer

GLUTEN-FREE
VEGETARIAN
NUT-FREE
FREEZER-FRIENDLY

2 pounds russet (baking) potatoes (2 large or 3 small)

2 tablespoons butter

⅓ cup milk

1 teaspoon salt

Ground black pepper

¾ cup freshly grated Cheddar cheese

Are you ready to kick up classic mashed potatoes a few notches? You're going to love this version with a layer of warm toasted cheese on top—yum! And since it uses unpeeled potatoes, you get an extra nutritional punch.

1. Bring a medium saucepan of water to a boil over high heat. Scrub the potatoes with water and a bristled brush (no need to peel!). Cut into 1- to 2-inch dice, add them to the water, and cook until tender when pierced with a fork, 15 to 20 minutes. Drain.

2. In a large bowl, puree the potatoes with an electric mixer or hand masher. Mix in the butter, milk, salt, and pepper to taste until thoroughly combined and smooth, taking care not to overmix.

3. Position a rack 3 to 4 inches from the broiler element and turn the broiler to high. Transfer the potatoes to a baking dish and top with an even layer of the Cheddar. Place the dish right under the broiler until the cheese is melted and just begins to brown (be sure to watch it closely!), 3 to 5 minutes. Serve warm.

SHOPPING LIST		PANTRY AND FRIDGE CHECKLIST
2 pounds russet potatoes (2 large or 3 small)	$2.58	2 tablespoons butter
One 2-pint container milk	$0.99	Salt and pepper
One 8-ounce block Cheddar cheese	$3.89	**INGREDIENTS LEFT OVER**
TOTAL	**$7.46**	Cheddar cheese
COST PER SERVING	**$1.24**	Milk

LISA'S TIP: If you want to make this dish ahead of time (which is especially helpful if you're hosting the holidays!), complete steps 1 and 2 in advance and refrigerate the mashed potatoes overnight. Heat the potatoes at 350°F for 20 to 30 minutes to reheat them all the way through, then do the last broiling step with the cheese.

snacks and appetizers

snack and appetizer recipes

Oatmeal Cookie Energy Bites

My older daughter can put away some of these oatmeal cookie bites like it's her job. Gymnastics helps her keep active, which means she's often super hungry, and I love to have these on hand for when she needs a snack.

In a large bowl, combine all the ingredients and stir until well mixed. Roll into 18 bite-size balls with wet hands to keep the mixture from sticking to you (or use a melon scooper to help). Store in the refrigerator for up to 1 week.

SHOPPING LIST		PANTRY AND FRIDGE CHECKLIST
One 1-pound bag rolled oats	$1.79	¼ cup pure maple syrup
One 16-ounce jar peanut butter	$2.67	½ teaspoon ground cinnamon
One 12-ounce box raisins	$2.49	**INGREDIENTS LEFT OVER**
TOTAL	**$6.95**	Rolled oats
COST PER SERVING (2 balls)	**$0.77**	Peanut butter
		Raisins

Difficulty: Super easy
Prep time: 10 minutes
Cook time: N/A
Makes eighteen 1½-inch bites

GLUTEN-FREE (IF GLUTEN-FREE OATS ARE USED)
DAIRY-FREE
VEGETARIAN

1½ cups rolled oats

⅔ cup peanut butter

½ cup raisins

¼ cup pure maple syrup

½ teaspoon ground cinnamon

"I've tried other homemade energy snacks and been disappointed, so I was skeptical when I got this recipe, but both my husband and I love them. I will definitely make them again!"

—Cinda O'Keefe, recipe tester

Lemon and Feta Quinoa Cakes

Difficulty: Medium
Prep time: 10 to 15 minutes
Cook time: 14 to 16 minutes (if made in 2 batches)
Makes fifteen 3-inch cakes

VEGETARIAN
NUT-FREE
FREEZER-FRIENDLY

3 cups cooked quinoa

2 eggs

¾ teaspoon salt

¼ cup whole wheat flour

Grated zest of ½ lemon

1 tablespoon fresh lemon juice

½ cup fresh parsley leaves, chopped

½ cup crumbled feta cheese

Olive oil, for cooking

These cakes are so filling and flavorful and can really serve as a snack, side item, or appetizer (just make them a little smaller to be bite-size). And be sure to break up some of the leftovers over a big salad for lunch the next day. The options are endless!

1.   In a large bowl, thoroughly combine the quinoa, eggs, salt, flour, lemon zest, lemon juice, parsley, and feta. With wet hands, form the quinoa mixture into 15 patties about 3 inches wide and 1 inch thick.

2.   In a large sauté pan with a tight-fitting lid, heat a thin layer of olive oil over medium-low heat. Add half the cakes, cover, and cook until the bottoms are browned, 6 to 8 minutes. Flip and repeat, adding more olive oil if necessary to keep the pan from becoming dry. Repeat to make the rest of the cakes.

3.   Serve warm and store leftovers in the fridge for up to 5 days. They are great to have on hand!

SHOPPING LIST		PANTRY AND FRIDGE CHECKLIST
One 12-ounce box quinoa	$3.99	Salt
Half dozen eggs	$0.85	¼ cup whole wheat flour
1 lemon	$0.65	Parsley (garden)
One 4-ounce tub crumbled feta cheese	$2.49	Olive oil, for cooking
TOTAL	**$7.98**	**INGREDIENTS LEFT OVER**
COST PER SERVING (3 cakes)	**$1.60**	Quinoa
		Eggs
		Lemon

Flavored Toast—Three Ways

Pictured clockwise from top: Garlic Toast (opposite), Maple-Cinnamon Toast (opposite), and Cumin Cheese Toast (page 144)

Flavored toasts are a super simple and filling snack that can be customized many different ways, and they may be called "toasts," but they're great way beyond breakfast. The savory ones are wonderful (and budget-friendly) snacks or side items, and I think my broiler trick beats a standard toaster oven any day!

Difficulty: Super easy
Prep time: 5 minutes
Cook time: 1 to 2 minutes
Makes 4 servings

**GLUTEN-FREE (IF GLUTEN-FREE
  BREAD IS USED)**
VEGETARIAN
NUT-FREE

GARLIC TOAST

2 tablespoons butter, at room temperature

4 large slices whole wheat sandwich bread

½ teaspoon garlic powder/ granules

1. Position an oven rack just below the heating element and pre-heat the broiler to high.

2. Spread the butter on one side of the bread and evenly sprinkle on the garlic powder. Place the slices directly on the top oven rack (no baking sheet) and broil until bubbling and golden brown around the edges, 1 to 2 minutes. Watch closely!

SHOPPING LIST		PANTRY AND FRIDGE CHECKLIST
1 loaf high-quality 100% whole wheat bread	$4.99	2 tablespoons butter
		½ teaspoon garlic powder
TOTAL	**$4.99**	
COST PER SERVING	**$1.25**	**INGREDIENTS LEFT OVER** Bread

MAPLE-CINNAMON TOAST

2 tablespoons butter, at room temperature

1 teaspoon ground cinnamon

1 teaspoon pure maple syrup

4 large slices whole wheat sandwich bread

1. Position an oven rack just below the heating element and pre-heat the broiler to high.

2. In a small bowl, mix the butter, cinnamon, and maple syrup until well combined. Evenly spread on one side of the bread slices. Place the slices directly on the top oven rack (no baking sheet) and broil until bubbling and golden brown around the edges, 1 to 2 minutes. Watch closely!

SHOPPING LIST		PANTRY AND FRIDGE CHECKLIST
1 loaf high-quality 100% whole wheat bread	$4.99	2 tablespoons butter 1 teaspoon ground cinnamon 1 teaspoon pure maple syrup
TOTAL	**$4.99**	
COST PER SERVING	**$1.25**	**INGREDIENTS LEFT OVER** Bread

(continues on next page)

4 large slices whole wheat sandwich bread

1 cup shredded Monterey Jack cheese

½ teaspoon ground cumin

CUMIN CHEESE TOAST

1. Position an oven rack just below the heating element and preheat the broiler to high.

2. Sprinkle the cheese on one side of the bread slices and evenly sprinkle the cumin on top. Place the slices directly on the top oven rack (no baking sheet) and broil until bubbling and golden brown around the edges, 1 to 2 minutes. Watch closely!

SHOPPING LIST		PANTRY AND FRIDGE CHECKLIST
1 loaf high-quality 100% whole wheat bread	$4.99	½ teaspoon ground cumin
One 8-ounce block Monterey Jack cheese	$3.89	**INGREDIENTS LEFT OVER**
TOTAL	**$8.88**	Bread
COST PER SERVING	**$2.22**	Monterey Jack cheese

Pictured: Cumin Cheese Toast

LISA'S TIP: I call these "toasts," but they come out toasty around the edges and delightfully warm and gooey in the center. If you prefer your toast to be crispy all the way through, you can run the bread through your toaster first.

Easy Green Smoothie

Smoothies are a great way to meet your fruit and veggie quota for the day! It takes no time at all to blend a few ingredients together, but you could even make this a day in advance if you really want to set yourself up for success on a busy weekday. We also sometimes freeze our smoothies in silicone ice-pop molds (which I found online) to send in the lunch box or enjoy on a hot summer day.

Blend all the ingredients until smooth. Serve immediately, refrigerate for up to 24 hours, or freeze in ice-pop molds.

Difficulty: Super easy
Prep time: 5 to 10 minutes
Cook time: N/A
Makes 4 servings
Special tools: Blender

GLUTEN-FREE
DAIRY-FREE
VEGETARIAN
NUT-FREE
FREEZER-FRIENDLY

2 cups fresh kale leaves (big stems and center ribs removed)

1½ cups frozen peach slices

1½ cups frozen pineapple chunks

2 ripe bananas (the riper they are, the sweeter the smoothie)

2 cups coconut water or plain water

SHOPPING LIST		PANTRY AND FRIDGE CHECKLIST
1 bunch kale, any variety	$1.99	N/A
One 20-ounce bag frozen sliced peaches	$3.85	
6-ounce bag frozen pineapple chunks	$3.59	**INGREDIENTS LEFT OVER**
2 ripe bananas	$0.40	Kale
One 16.9-ounce carton coconut water	$2.49	Frozen peaches
		Frozen pineapple
TOTAL	**$12.32**	
COST PER SERVING	**$3.08**	

Chili-Lime-Watermelon Skewers

Even hard-core watermelon fans usually only eat it plain. But you can totally spice up your watermelon by adding extra flavors or mixing it with other ingredients (such as feta cheese and mint) to make a refreshing salad. This is one of our favorite ways to change up watermelon, and it's especially great paired with Mexican food and margaritas!

Cut the watermelon into 1- to 1½-inch cubes and thread them onto skewers. Drizzle the lime juice over the skewers and sprinkle the chili powder and salt over the top. Serve within a few hours.

Difficulty: Super easy
Prep time: 15 minutes
Cook time: N/A
Makes ten 8-inch skewers
Special tools: Ten 8-inch
   wooden skewers

GLUTEN-FREE
DAIRY-FREE
VEGETARIAN
NUT-FREE

1 small watermelon (4 to 4½ pounds)
Juice of 1 lime
½ teaspoon chili powder
⅛ teaspoon salt

SHOPPING LIST		PANTRY AND FRIDGE CHECKLIST
One small watermelon		½ teaspoon chili powder
(4 to 4½ pounds)	$4.99	Salt
1 lime	$0.25	
TOTAL	**$5.24**	**INGREDIENTS LEFT OVER**
COST PER SERVING		N/A
(2 skewers)	**$1.05**	

Whole Wheat Banana (Nut) Muffins

Difficulty: Easy

Prep time: 15 minutes

Cook time: 18 to 20 minutes for standard muffins, 12 to 14 minutes for mini-muffins

Makes 12 regular muffins or 36 mini-muffins

Special tools: Muffin tin (regular or mini) and liners

DAIRY-FREE (IF COCONUT OIL IS SUBSTITUTED FOR THE BUTTER 1:1)

VEGETARIAN

NUT-FREE (IF WALNUTS ARE OMITTED)

FREEZER-FRIENDLY

1½ cups whole wheat flour

¾ teaspoon baking soda

½ teaspoon salt

¼ teaspoon baking powder

2 eggs, whisked

1 stick (4 ounces) butter, melted

⅓ cup pure maple syrup

2 very ripe bananas, peeled (the riper the bananas, the sweeter the muffins)

½ cup chopped walnuts (optional)

I've always had a thing for banana-nut muffins, but it wasn't until we cut out all highly processed food that I realized that standard muffins are kind of like cupcakes minus the icing. They typically call for all-purpose white flour and refined sugar—and lots of it. Some recipes call for as much as a cup (or even more) of sugar in a batch of 12 muffins—as much as some cupcake recipes! The great news is that if you use whole-grain flour and a smaller amount of (a more natural) sweetener, muffins can actually be the snack and breakfast food they were meant to be.

1. Preheat the oven to 350°F. Line a muffin tin with paper or silicone liners.

2. In a large bowl, whisk the flour, baking soda, salt, and baking powder. Make a well (hole) in the center of the flour mixture and pour in the eggs, melted butter, and maple syrup. Mix with a fork until the batter just comes together.

3. In a small bowl, mash the bananas with the back of a fork. Carefully fold the bananas and walnuts (if using) into the muffin batter and divide evenly among the 12 muffin cups (or 36 mini-muffin cups).

4. Bake until the muffins begin to brown on top and a toothpick inserted in the center of a muffin comes out clean, 18 to 20 minutes for standard muffins or 12 to 14 minutes for mini-muffins.

LISA'S TIP: I love to store mine on a pretty cake platter (with a lid) on the kitchen counter. The muffins can be stored at room temperature for 3 to 4 days, then transfer to the fridge or freezer (if they last that long)!

SHOPPING LIST

One 2-pound bag whole wheat flour	$3.49
One 8-ounce box butter	$2.69
Half dozen eggs	$0.85
One 8-ounce jar pure maple syrup	$4.99
2 bananas	$0.40
TOTAL	**$12.42**
COST PER SERVING (1 regular muffin)	**$1.03**

PANTRY AND FRIDGE CHECKLIST

¾ teaspoon baking soda
¼ teaspoon baking powder
Salt

INGREDIENTS LEFT OVER

Flour
Eggs
Butter
Maple syrup

Fruit Leather—Two Ways

Reminiscent of fruit roll-ups, these homemade fruit leathers are simple to make and much better for you. You can feel good about offering these instead of the store-bought version from our childhood, which contains corn syrup and artificial dyes, among other unwanted additives.

1. Preheat the oven to 200°F, using convection heat if you have it. Line a 13 x 18-inch rimmed baking sheet with parchment paper. (Alternatively, a dehydrator can be used following manufacturer directions.)

2. To make either recipe, blend the frozen fruit, maple syrup, and water until smooth.

3. Pour the fruit puree onto the prepared baking sheet and use a spatula to spread it into an even layer (jiggle the pan a bit to make sure it's even).

4. Bake until the fruit has completely dried out and is no longer wet to the touch, anywhere between 2 and 4 hours (ovens will vary), checking on it every 20 to 30 minutes near the end. When you figure out the timing for fruit leathers in your oven, you'll be set for next time.

5. Let the fruit leather cool completely at room temperature so it can soften (it may seem hard right out of the oven). Cut it into strips, including the parchment paper.

6. When you're ready to eat it, peel off the parchment and serve. The fruit leather can be stored at room temperature for a couple of weeks.

Difficulty: Easy
Prep time: 10 minutes
Cook time: 3 to 4 hours (hands-off)
Makes about fourteen 9-inch strips
Special tools: 13 x 18-inch rimmed baking sheet, parchment paper, and blender

GLUTEN-FREE
DAIRY-FREE
VEGETARIAN
NUT-FREE
FREEZER-FRIENDLY

TRIPLE BERRY

3 cups frozen mixed berries (strawberries, blueberries, raspberries, and/or blackberries)

3 tablespoons pure maple syrup

½ cup water

TROPICAL SUNRISE

1½ cups frozen peach slices

1½ cups frozen pineapple chunks

3 tablespoons pure maple syrup

1 cup water

(continues on next page)

SHOPPING LIST		PANTRY AND FRIDGE CHECKLIST
Two 10-ounce bags frozen fruit (berries or pineapple and peaches)	$6.78	3 tablespoons pure maple syrup
TOTAL	**$6.78**	**INGREDIENTS LEFT OVER**
COST PER SERVING (1 strip)	**$0.48**	Frozen fruit

"I used this recipe as my nutrition for my half marathon. It was perfect, and I'm going to make it again for my upcoming marathon."

—Anne Sparks, recipe tester
(I had little ones in mind when I developed this recipe, but loved this feedback!)

LISA'S TIP: It can take a little practice to get used to how this recipe will work in your oven, but once you get over that hump it'll be super easy the next time. It's definitely worth the effort!

Easy Pickle Dip

Dips are obviously a staple at almost any social gathering, but most of the ones I come across are honestly best when served with deep-fried potato chips—a real food no-no! This dip was inspired by my friend Emily and one of the things I love about it, other than the yummy pickle flavor, is the fact that it pairs perfectly with whole-grain pretzels as the dippers instead of chips.

In a large bowl, combine all the ingredients and stir to blend. Serve with whole-grain pretzels or store in the fridge for up to 5 days.

Difficulty: Super easy
Prep time: 5 to 10 minutes
Cook time: N/A
Makes 8 to 10 servings

GLUTEN-FREE
VEGETARIAN
NUT-FREE

One 16-ounce container sour cream

4 ounces cream cheese, at room temperature

1 cup finely diced dill pickle (or relish)

2 tablespoons pickle (or relish) juice

1 teaspoon garlic powder

¼ teaspoon dried dill

¼ teaspoon salt

SHOPPING LIST		PANTRY AND FRIDGE CHECKLIST
One 16-ounce container sour cream	$1.38	¼ teaspoon dried dill
One 8-ounce block cream cheese	$2.00	1 teaspoon garlic powder
One 16-ounce jar dill pickles	$1.79	Salt
TOTAL	**$5.17**	**INGREDIENTS LEFT OVER**
COST PER SERVING	**$0.52**	Cream cheese
		Pickles

"I was skeptical at first, but pretzels and this dip are an amazing combination!"

—Amy Coe Goins, recipe tester

LISA'S TIP: When shopping for pickles, be sure to avoid brands that use artificial food dyes (it's more common than you'd think!) or added refined sugar.

Roasted Rosemary Almonds

When it was my turn to host my neighborhood book club, I made a variety of easy appetizers (such as deviled eggs and Caprese salad) and decided to throw in a batch of these almonds as well. This was during the testing phase of my cookbook so no one outside of my family had tried them yet. I didn't say a word about the recipe being new, and, much to my delight (completely unsolicited), it was the one appetizer my neighbors were unanimously raving about. Needless to say, this one made it into the book!

1. Preheat the oven to 375°F.

2. Toss all the ingredients on a rimmed baking sheet and bake until the almonds are toasted and slightly darker in color, 10 to 15 minutes, stirring every 5 minutes or so to prevent burning.

3. Let cool, then store in an airtight container at room temperature. Shake before serving to mix the rosemary back in (it will settle in the container).

Difficulty: Super easy
Prep time: 5 minutes
Cook time: 12 to 15 minutes
Makes 1 cup
Special tools: Rimmed
baking sheet

GLUTEN-FREE
DAIRY-FREE
VEGETARIAN

1 cup whole raw almonds

1 tablespoon olive oil

1 tablespoon chopped fresh rosemary

¼ teaspoon salt

⅛ teaspoon cayenne pepper

"This would make a *terrific* hostess or holiday gift!"

—Meghan Alpern,
recipe tester

SHOPPING LIST		PANTRY AND FRIDGE CHECKLIST
One 8-ounce bag whole raw almonds	$5.99	Rosemary (garden)
TOTAL	**$5.99**	1 tablespoon olive oil
COST PER SERVING		Salt
(¼ cup)	**$1.50**	⅛ teaspoon cayenne pepper
		INGREDIENTS LEFT OVER
		Almonds

The Best Oven-Baked Chicken Wings!

I don't typically call for special "gourmet" ingredients, but I'm making an exception here, and for very good reason. These wings are to die for, and that's because the smoked sea salt mimics the flavor you'd get cooking them all day in a smoker. And you'll find lots of good ways to use the leftover smoked salt; deviled eggs would be a great place to start.

1. Line a 13 x 18-inch rimmed baking sheet with foil and set the cooling rack on top. Position a rack in the middle of the oven and preheat the oven to 425°F.

2. Pour the maple syrup into a large bowl. Add the wings and mix with your hands to coat the wings evenly. Arrange the wings on the rack, thick-skinned side down.

3. Designate one hand as your "dry hand" (for the spice mixture) and one as your "wet hand" (for the raw chicken). In a small bowl, use your dry hand to mix together the black pepper, smoked salt, paprika, thyme, oregano, and cayenne. Evenly sprinkle about half the spice mixture over the wings. With your wet hand, press the spice rub into the wings, then flip them over (we want the thick-skinned side up during baking for extra crispiness). Evenly sprinkle the remaining spice mixture on the wings with your dry hand.

4. Set the pan on the middle oven rack and bake until golden brown and crispy, about 45 minutes. Serve warm or at room temperature.

Difficulty: Easy
Prep time: 15 minutes
Cook time: 45 minutes
   (hands-off)
Makes 6 to 8 servings
Special tools: 13 x 18-inch
   rimmed baking sheet and
   cooling rack

GLUTEN-FREE
DAIRY-FREE
NUT-FREE
FREEZER-FRIENDLY

1 tablespoon pure maple syrup or honey

3 pounds chicken wings (about 3 dozen), patted dry with a paper towel

2½ teaspoons ground black pepper

1½ teaspoons smoked sea salt (can substitute regular sea salt, but you'd be missing out!)

1 teaspoon paprika

1 teaspoon dried thyme

½ teaspoon dried oregano

½ teaspoon cayenne pepper

SHOPPING LIST		PANTRY AND FRIDGE CHECKLIST	INGREDIENTS LEFT OVER
3 pounds chicken wings (about 3 dozen)	$8.07	1 tablespoon pure maple syrup or honey	Smoked sea salt (lucky you!)
One 2.4-ounce jar (applewood) smoked sea salt	$4.17*	2½ teaspoons black pepper 1 teaspoon dried thyme	
TOTAL	**$12.24**	1 teaspoon paprika	
COST PER SERVING	**$1.53**	½ teaspoon dried oregano	
*price on Amazon		½ teaspoon cayenne pepper	

CHAPTER 6

*simple
dinners*

simple dinner recipes

The Easiest Spinach Lasagna

Okay, so I admit it. Frozen spinach is super convenient to use in recipes, but I can sometimes taste the difference between frozen and fresh (and I don't mean in a good way). So I was pleasantly surprised when I tried mixing it directly into the cheesy goodness of this spinach lasagna and seriously could not taste any frozen "flavors" at all. My family devoured it for both dinner and lunch the next day. Leftovers are the best when you're cooking everything from scratch!

1. Preheat the oven to 375°F.

2. In a large bowl, mix the ricotta, mozzarella, ¾ cup of the Parmesan, the spinach, egg (if using), salt, and pepper to taste.

3. Spread ¾ cup of the marinara sauce in a 9 x 13-inch baking dish, followed by a layer of a few of the noodles, then one-third of the cheese mixture, followed by ¾ cup marinara. Repeat until all the ingredients are used, ending with the sauce.

4. Top with the remaining ¼ cup Parmesan, cover with foil, and bake for 30 minutes. Remove the foil and bake until the noodles have completely softened, 20 to 25 minutes. Let rest for 5 minutes, serve warm, and enjoy!

Difficulty: Easy
Prep time: 15 minutes
Cook time: 50 to 55 minutes (hands-off)
Makes 6 servings
Special tools: 9 x 13-inch baking dish

VEGETARIAN
NUT-FREE
FREEZER-FRIENDLY

One 15-ounce container ricotta cheese

8 ounces mozzarella cheese, shredded

1 cup freshly grated Parmesan cheese

One 10-ounce package frozen chopped spinach, thawed and squeezed dry

1 egg (optional)

¼ teaspoon salt

Ground black pepper

3 cups marinara sauce, homemade or good-quality store bought

8 ounces 100% whole-grain no-boil lasagna noodles (or regular lasagna noodles, boiled according to package directions)

SHOPPING LIST		TOTAL	$15.38
		COST PER SERVING	$2.56
One 15-ounce container ricotta cheese	$2.49		
One 8-ounce block mozzarella cheese	$3.89	**PANTRY AND FRIDGE CHECKLIST**	
One 6-ounce tub freshly grated Parmesan cheese	$3.99	Salt and pepper	
One 10-ounce package frozen chopped spinach	$1.49	**INGREDIENTS LEFT OVER**	
One 24-ounce jar marinara sauce	$1.63	Parmesan cheese	
One 13.25-ounce box 100% whole-grain no-boil or other lasagna noodles	$1.89	Whole-grain lasagna noodles	

Braised Chicken and Carrots with Rosemary Gravy

Difficulty: Easy
Prep time: 15 minutes
Cook time: 14 to 16 minutes
Makes 4 servings

NUT-FREE
FREEZER-FRIENDLY

1¼ pounds boneless, skinless chicken thighs

½ cup whole wheat flour

3 tablespoons butter

1 pound carrots (about 6), peeled and cut into large dice

1 cup chicken or veggie broth

¼ cup heavy cream

Leaves from 1 fresh rosemary sprig, chopped

½ teaspoon salt

Ground black pepper

Suggested accompaniments: Mashed potatoes or wild rice blend

My family loves Apple-Glazed Pork Chops (page 176) so much that I knew I had to come up with another recipe using that same concept. I mean, it's hard to turn down homemade gravy! So I simply replaced the pork with chicken, the apples with carrots, the apple juice with broth, and the sage with rosemary and we have ourselves a whole new dinner using the same easy cooking method.

1. Dredge the chicken in the flour until well coated in all the creases.

2. In a large skillet, melt the butter over medium-high heat. Add the chicken and carrots and cook until the chicken is golden brown on both sides, 2 to 3 minutes per side, cooking in batches if necessary.

3. Pour in the broth, cover, bring to a low simmer, and cook until the chicken is done (no longer pink in the middle) and the carrots are tender when pierced with a fork, 8 to 10 minutes. Uncover the pan, increase the heat to medium, and cook for 2 to 3 minutes to thicken the sauce while scraping the browned bits off the bottom.

4. Stir in the cream, rosemary, salt, and pepper to taste. Serve warm over mashed potatoes or wild rice.

SHOPPING LIST		PANTRY AND FRIDGE CHECKLIST
1¼ pounds boneless, skinless chicken thighs	$3.36	3 tablespoons butter
One 2-pound bag whole wheat flour	$3.49	Salt and pepper
1 pound carrots	$0.99	Rosemary (garden)
One 14.5-ounce can chicken or veggie broth	$1.37	**INGREDIENTS LEFT OVER**
½ pint heavy cream	$2.29	Flour
TOTAL	**$11.50**	Broth
COST PER SERVING	**$2.89**	Heavy cream

Simple Walnut-Crusted Salmon

This tops the list as one of the fastest and easiest dinner dishes of all time. As I've said before, one of my favorite things about seafood is how fast it cooks, and the walnut crust in this recipe adds just minutes to the prep time. Plus, it was a big hit with my kids—double score!

1. Preheat the oven to 400°F. Oil a baking sheet.

2. Place the salmon fillets skin side down on the oiled pan.

3. In a food processor, combine the breadcrumbs, walnuts, mustard, and honey. Process until well combined, scraping the sides as necessary.

4. Use a spatula to spread the walnut crust in an even layer on top of the salmon. Bake until the salmon is a little golden brown on top and cooked (light pink and flaky) all the way through, 12 to 15 minutes depending on the thickness of the fish.

Difficulty: Super easy
Prep time: 10 to 15 minutes
Cook time: 12 to 15 minutes
    (hands-off)
Makes 4 servings
Special tools: Food processor
    and baking sheet

GLUTEN-FREE (IF GLUTEN-FREE
    BREADCRUMBS ARE USED)
DAIRY-FREE

Oil, for the pan
1 pound wild-caught salmon
fillets, thawed if frozen
¼ cup whole wheat
breadcrumbs
¼ cup chopped walnuts
1 tablespoon Dijon or regular
mustard
1 tablespoon honey

SHOPPING LIST		PANTRY AND FRIDGE CHECKLIST

1 pound wild-caught
  salmon fillets
	$9.99	1 tablespoon Dijon or regular
		  mustard

One 15-ounce canister
  whole wheat
  breadcrumbs
	$2.89	1 tablespoon honey
		Olive oil

One 4-ounce bag chopped walnuts	$2.99	**INGREDIENTS LEFT OVER**
TOTAL	**$15.87**	Breadcrumbs
COST PER SERVING	**$3.97**	Walnuts

Easy Chinese Chicken

Difficulty: Easy
Prep time: 15 minutes
Cook time: 10 to 15 minutes
Makes 4 or 5 servings

DAIRY-FREE
NUT-FREE
FREEZER-FRIENDLY

CHICKEN

¼ cup soy sauce

¼ cup water

1½ pounds boneless, skinless chicken thighs, cut into 2-inch cubes

1 cup whole wheat flour

4 tablespoons coconut oil

SAUCE

2 garlic cloves, minced

1 teaspoon grated fresh ginger

1 teaspoon red pepper flakes (½ teaspoon if you prefer it mild)

2 tablespoons rice vinegar

2 tablespoons honey

¼ cup soy sauce

½ cup water

Say goodbye to questionable Chinese takeout and make this super-easy dish instead. It would be great served over brown rice with a green veggie on the side, such as raw sugar snap peas or sautéed bok choy.

1. To make the chicken: In a shallow dish, combine the soy sauce and water. Add the chicken and marinate for at least 10 to 15 minutes at room temperature or up to a few hours in the refrigerator.

2. Place the flour on a plate. Remove the chicken from the marinade and roll the pieces around in the flour until all sides are coated.

3. In a large skillet, melt the coconut oil over medium heat. Add the chicken and cook until golden brown all over and cooked through, 6 to 8 minutes. Remove the chicken to a plate, leaving the flavorful bits in the pan.

4. To make the sauce: In the same pan over medium heat, cook the garlic, ginger, and pepper flakes for 30 to 60 seconds, then whisk in the vinegar, honey, soy sauce, and water and bring to a boil. Cook, scraping up the browned bits in the bottom of the pan, until the liquid begins to thicken, 2 to 3 minutes. Add the chicken, stir to coat it in the sauce, and serve warm.

SHOPPING LIST		PANTRY AND FRIDGE CHECKLIST
One 15-ounce bottle soy sauce	$2.49	¼ cup coconut oil
1½ pounds boneless, skinless chicken thighs	$4.03	1 teaspoon red pepper flakes
One 2-pound bag whole wheat flour	$3.49	2 tablespoons rice vinegar
1 garlic head	$0.50	2 tablespoons honey
2 ounces fresh ginger	$0.63	**INGREDIENTS LEFT OVER**
TOTAL	**$11.14**	Soy sauce
COST PER SERVING	**$2.23**	Flour
		Garlic
		Ginger

LISA'S TIP: I used chicken thighs in this recipe because they are a better deal (and I often think they taste better, too)! But you could substitute chicken breasts if you'd prefer.

Cheesy Zucchini "Meatballs"

I'm all about increasing our veggie consumption without having to try too hard, so I love this twist on one of our most favorite family meals, spaghetti and meatballs. Now, we still love our regular meatballs made with meat, but just to switch things up (and make sure we get a good dose of veggies), we enjoy this new zucchini version as well.

1. Preheat the oven to 425°F. Grease a large baking sheet with oil.

2. Shred the zucchini using a food processor's shredding disk or a hand grater. Use a clean kitchen towel to squeeze out as much liquid from the zucchini as you can (discard the liquid).

3. In a large bowl, mix the zucchini, eggs, breadcrumbs, Parmesan, basil, garlic, and salt until well combined.

4. To form the "meatballs," take a handful of the zucchini mixture, shove one of the mozzarella cubes in the middle, then form it into a "meatball" with the mozzarella completely covered in the zucchini mixture. Squeeze the "meatball" together gently but firmly to get rid of any remaining excess liquid and set it on the prepared pan. Repeat to make 12 to 14 "meatballs."

5. Bake until golden brown on the bottom, 14 to 16 minutes.

Difficulty: Medium
Prep time: 20 minutes
Cook time: 14 to 16 minutes
  (hands-off)
Makes 4 servings
Special tools: Baking sheet
  and food processor (not
  necessary, but helpful)

VEGETARIAN
NUT-FREE
FREEZER-FRIENDLY

Oil, for the baking sheet

3 medium zucchini (about
1½ pounds), ends trimmed

2 eggs, lightly beaten

⅓ cup whole wheat
breadcrumbs, store bought or
homemade (see Tip, page 212)

⅓ cup freshly grated Parmesan
cheese

2 tablespoons chopped fresh
basil

2 garlic cloves, minced

½ teaspoon salt

4 ounces mozzarella cheese,
cut into 12 equal-size cubes

Suggested accompaniments:
Whole wheat noodles, marinara
sauce, and extra grated
Parmesan to go on top

SHOPPING LIST		PANTRY AND FRIDGE CHECKLIST
One 8-ounce block mozzarella cheese	$3.89	Basil (garden)
3 medium zucchini (about 1½ pounds)	$2.54	Salt
Half dozen eggs	$0.85	Oil, for greasing
One 15-ounce canister whole wheat breadcrumbs	$2.89	**INGREDIENTS LEFT OVER**
One 6-ounce tub freshly grated Parmesan cheese	$3.99	Mozzarella cheese
1 garlic head	$0.50	Eggs
		Breadcrumbs
TOTAL	**$14.66**	Parmesan cheese
COST PER SERVING		Garlic
(3 "meatballs")	**$3.67**	

Asian Chicken Lettuce Cups

Difficulty: Easy
Prep time: 15 minutes
Cook time: 10 to 12 minutes
Makes 4 servings

GLUTEN-FREE (IF GLUTEN-FREE SOY SAUCE IS USED)
DAIRY-FREE
NUT-FREE

2 tablespoons coconut oil

½ teaspoon red pepper flakes

1 large sweet potato (12 to 14 ounces), peeled and cut into ¼- to ½-inch dice

1½ pounds boneless, skinless chicken breasts, cut into 1-inch dice

One 8-ounce can diced water chestnuts, drained

1 tablespoon minced fresh ginger

2 garlic cloves, minced

2 tablespoons soy sauce

1 tablespoon toasted sesame oil

1 tablespoon rice vinegar

Bibb or iceberg lettuce leaves, for serving

½ cup fresh cilantro leaves

The first time I got my kids to eat lettuce was by wrapping some good stuff inside and serving it as a small wrap. I told them if they wanted the filling they had to eat the lettuce on the outside as well, and it worked! Don't ever give up on trying to get your kids to eat new things. It can feel like a lot of work and effort at the time, but it's always worth it in the end.

1. In a large skillet, melt 1 tablespoon of the coconut oil over medium heat. Add the pepper flakes and sweet potato. Cook, stirring occasionally with a spatula, until the potato just starts to brown, 3 to 4 minutes.

2. Add the remaining 1 tablespoon coconut oil, the chicken, and the water chestnuts and cook, stirring occasionally with a spatula, until the chicken is cooked through, 4 to 5 minutes. Add the ginger and garlic and cook, stirring, for 1 minute.

3. Remove from the heat and mix in the soy sauce, sesame oil, and vinegar.

4. Serve on lettuce leaves and top with cilantro.

SHOPPING LIST		PANTRY AND FRIDGE CHECKLIST
1 large sweet potato	$0.65	2 tablespoons coconut oil
1½ pounds boneless, skinless chicken breasts	$5.24	2 tablespoons soy sauce
		1 tablespoon toasted sesame oil
One 8-ounce can diced water chestnuts	$0.99	1 tablespoon rice vinegar
1 garlic head	$0.50	½ teaspoon red pepper flakes
2 ounces fresh ginger	$0.63	Cilantro (garden)
1 head Bibb or iceberg lettuce	$0.99	**INGREDIENTS LEFT OVER**
TOTAL	**$9.00**	Garlic
COST PER SERVING	**$2.25**	Ginger

Sydney's Veggie Cream Pasta

One summer when our family rented a house in Maine for a week I decided that each person would be assigned a night to cook a dinner of their choice. Mommy wanted to be on vacation, too, after all! The dinners that my daughters came up with ended up being so good that I thought they both deserved a spot in my newest cookbook. Here is Sydney's, and you can find Sienna's on page 195.

1. In a large skillet, melt the butter over medium heat. Add the zucchini, bell pepper, mushroom, and jalapeño and cook, stirring occasionally, until tender, 5 to 6 minutes.

2. Reduce the heat to medium-low. Pour in the cream, sprinkle in the Parmesan, and season with salt and pepper to taste. Bring to a simmer to thicken slightly, 3 to 4 minutes. Serve warm over the cooked noodles, with a sprinkling of parsley if desired.

SHOPPING LIST		PANTRY AND FRIDGE CHECKLIST
1 zucchini (about 12 ounces)	$1.27	2 tablespoons butter
1 green bell pepper	$0.99	Salt and pepper
1 portobello mushroom (1 ounce)	$0.62	**INGREDIENTS LEFT OVER**
1 jalapeño pepper	$0.31	Jalapeño
½ pint heavy cream	$2.29	Parmesan cheese
One 6-ounce tub freshly grated Parmesan cheese	$3.99	Fettuccine
One 16-ounce box whole wheat fettuccine	$2.99	
TOTAL	**$12.46**	
COST PER SERVING	**$3.12**	

Difficulty: Easy
Prep time: 15 minutes
Cook time: 10 minutes (after the pasta is cooked)
Makes 4 servings

GLUTEN-FREE (IF GLUTEN-FREE PASTA IS USED)
VEGETARIAN
NUT-FREE

2 tablespoons butter

1 zucchini (about 12 ounces), cut into ½-inch dice

1 green bell pepper, cut into ½-inch squares

1 portobello mushroom (1 ounce), cut into ½-inch dice

½ jalapeño pepper, seeded and minced

1 cup heavy cream

⅔ cup freshly grated Parmesan cheese

Salt and ground black pepper

8 ounces whole wheat fettuccine, cooked according to package directions and drained

Suggested accompaniment: Fresh parsley leaves, for garnish (optional)

Apple-Glazed Pork Chops

Difficulty: Easy
Prep time: 10 to 15 minutes
Cook time: 12 to 15 minutes
Makes 4 servings

NUT-FREE

1 pound thin boneless pork chops

Salt and ground black pepper

½ cup whole wheat flour

3½ tablespoons butter

1 apple, unpeeled or peeled, cored, and cut into large dice

½ cup apple juice

½ cup water

Handful of fresh sage leaves, sliced

¼ cup heavy cream

This is the perfect weeknight comfort food to satisfy hungry bellies after a busy day. Pair with a green salad and some whole-grain wild rice and cleanup will be just as easy as preparation.

1. Sprinkle the pork chops with salt and pepper and coat all sides with the flour.

2. In your largest skillet, melt 3 tablespoons of the butter over medium heat. Add the pork chops and apple and cook until the chops are golden brown and cooked through in the middle (no longer pink), 2 to 3 minutes per side. Remove the pork chops to a plate and set aside.

3. With the heat still on medium, add the apple juice and water to the apples and boil, stirring, until reduced by half, about 5 minutes. The apple will still be in chunks but the sauce will be thicker.

4. Meanwhile, in a small skillet, melt the remaining ½ tablespoon butter over medium heat. Add the sage leaves and cook, stirring occasionally, until the butter just begins to brown. Watch closely because it can go from browned to burned very quickly. Immediately remove from the heat.

5. Stir the cream into the apple mixture and return the pork chops to the pan to reheat and coat them in sauce.

6. Sprinkle with the crispy sage leaves and serve.

SHOPPING LIST

1 pound thin boneless pork chops	$5.29
One 2-pound bag whole wheat flour	$3.49
1 apple	$0.75
One 11.5-ounce bottle apple juice	$1.89
½ pint heavy cream	$2.29
TOTAL	**$13.71**
COST PER SERVING	**$3.43**

PANTRY AND FRIDGE CHECKLIST

3½ tablespoons butter
Sage leaves (garden)
Salt and pepper

INGREDIENTS LEFT OVER

Apple juice
Heavy cream
Flour

Sausage and Pepper Tacos

I wasn't so sure about the concept of sausage in tacos, but I tried it myself and it's a winning combination! And best of all, it comes together as one of the easiest dinners, with very little cleanup involved.

1. Slice each sausage link down the middle lengthwise (this is easy with culinary shears). Place them cut side up in a large skillet over medium heat. Cook until golden brown on the bottom, 4 to 5 minutes.

2. Carefully turn over each piece of sausage and add the onion, bell pepper, and jalapeño to the pan. Cook, stirring the onion and peppers occasionally, until the sausage is cooked all the way through and the veggies have softened, 5 to 6 minutes.

3. Drain and discard any excess fat from the pan and stir in the lime juice. Serve warm with the accompaniments.

Difficulty: Super easy
Prep time: 10 to 15 minutes
Cook time: 10 to 12 minutes
Makes 4 servings

GLUTEN-FREE (IF GLUTEN-FREE TORTILLAS ARE USED)
DAIRY-FREE (IF SOUR CREAM AND CHEESE TOPPINGS ARE OMITTED)
NUT-FREE
FREEZER-FRIENDLY

4 raw kielbasa or bratwurst sausage links

1 yellow onion, thinly sliced

1 green bell pepper, cored, seeded, and thinly sliced

1 jalapeño pepper, seeded and minced

Juice of 1 lime

For serving: Whole-grain corn tortillas, grated Monterey Jack cheese, sour cream, and fresh cilantro

---

SHOPPING LIST

One 20-ounce package raw kielbasa or bratwurst sausage links	$5.99
1 onion (8 ounces)	$0.85
1 green bell pepper	$0.99
1 jalapeño pepper	$0.31
1 lime	$0.25
One 8-count package whole-grain corn tortillas	$1.89
One 8-ounce block Monterey Jack cheese	$3.89
One 8-ounce container sour cream	$0.99
TOTAL	**$15.16**
COST PER SERVING	**$3.79**

PANTRY AND FRIDGE CHECKLIST

Cilantro (garden)

INGREDIENTS LEFT OVER

Monterey Jack cheese
Sour cream

Mushroom and Brussels Sprouts Quesadillas

Difficulty: Medium
Prep time: 15 minutes
Cook time: 20 to 30 minutes
Makes 4 servings
Special tools: Food processor
(not necessary, but helpful)

GLUTEN-FREE (IF GLUTEN-FREE
TORTILLAS ARE USED)
VEGETARIAN
NUT-FREE
FREEZER-FRIENDLY

2 tablespoons butter, plus more
for cooking the quesadillas

2 shallots, finely diced

8 ounces Brussels sprouts,
trimmed and thinly sliced (can
use the slicing disk on a food
processor)

8 ounces mushrooms, thinly sliced

½ teaspoon chili powder

½ teaspoon dried oregano

½ teaspoon salt

8 whole wheat flour tortillas

2 cups shredded Monterey Jack
cheese

½ cup crumbled feta cheese

It's amazing how many different types of fresh produce you can put in a quesadilla and have it taste great. This might just be the perfect way to get your choosy little ones to eat some veggies they might have otherwise picked over!

1. In a large skillet, melt the 2 tablespoons butter over medium-low heat. Add the shallots and sprouts and cook, stirring occasionally, until they begin to soften, about 5 minutes. Add the mushrooms, chili powder, oregano, and salt and cook until the sprouts are tender, 3 to 5 minutes.

2. Lay out 4 of the tortillas. Evenly distribute the cheeses and veggie filling over the tortillas and cover with the remaining 4 tortillas.

3. Wipe out the skillet and place it over medium heat (or set an electric griddle to 350°F). Melt a big pat of butter in the pan. Working in batches, place the quesadillas in the pan. Smear another small pat of butter on top of each tortilla to help grease the pan when you flip the quesadillas over. Cook until the tortillas are golden brown, 3 to 5 minutes on each side. Transfer the cooked quesadillas to a large cutting board to cool while you cook the rest.

4. When the cheese is slightly cooled and set, cut each quesadilla into 4 or 6 slices. A pizza cutter makes this job easy.

SHOPPING LIST

2 shallots (¼ pound)	$1.25
One 8-ounce container Brussels sprouts	$2.79
8 ounces mushrooms	$2.34
One 8-ounce block Monterey Jack cheese	$3.89
One 4-ounce tub feta crumbles	$2.49
One 10-count package (16 ounces) whole wheat flour tortillas	$2.85
TOTAL	**$15.61**
COST PER SERVING	**$3.90**

PANTRY AND FRIDGE CHECKLIST

4 tablespoons (½ stick) butter
½ teaspoon chili powder
½ teaspoon dried oregano
Salt

INGREDIENTS LEFT OVER

Tortillas
Feta cheese

Jason's Carne Asada

My husband is the grill master at our house, and a huge fan of Mexican food—in fact, I think that's the one cuisine all four of us could eat indefinitely without ever getting tired of it. I'm excited to share his recipe for carne asada—the perfect dish to make when entertaining friends.

1. In a skillet, heat the olive oil over medium-low heat. Add the jalapeños, oregano, black pepper, and salt and sauté until the jalapeño is softened, about 2 minutes. Add the garlic and cook for 30 seconds, stirring frequently.

2. Pour the mixture into a glass bowl or small baking dish and mix in the lime juice. Add the steak and enough water to cover the meat fully. Marinate in the refrigerator for 20 to 30 minutes.

3. Preheat a grill to medium-high. Grill the steak to your desired doneness, 6 to 8 minutes per side for medium (still pink in the middle). Thinly slice against the grain and serve.

Difficulty: Easy
Prep time: 10 minutes +
   20 minutes to marinate
   (hands-off)
Cook time: 15 minutes
Makes 4 or 5 servings
Special tools: Outdoor grill

GLUTEN-FREE
DAIRY-FREE
NUT-FREE
FREEZER-FRIENDLY

3 tablespoons olive oil
2 jalapeño peppers, seeded and finely diced
1 teaspoon dried oregano
1 teaspoon ground black pepper
½ teaspoon salt
6 garlic cloves, minced
Juice of 2 limes
1½ pounds flank steak

Suggested accompaniments:
Whole-grain tortillas, salsa, pinto beans, and sliced green onions

SHOPPING LIST		PANTRY AND FRIDGE CHECKLIST
2 jalapeño peppers	$0.62	3 tablespoons olive oil
1 garlic head	$0.50	1 teaspoon dried oregano
2 limes	$0.50	Salt and pepper
1½ pounds flank steak	$10.49	
TOTAL	**$12.11**	**INGREDIENTS LEFT OVER**
COST PER SERVING	**$2.42**	Garlic

LISA'S TIP: We've learned from experience that sometimes the jalapeños from the store have some spice to them and sometimes they don't. So, if you enjoy a little kick, be on the lookout for peppers that are actually a little spicy! Maybe ask the produce manager to cut one up for you so you can taste test before you purchase.

Baked Shells with Ricotta and Marinara

Difficulty: Easy

Prep time: 15 to 20 minutes

Cook time: 20 to 25 minutes (hands-off)

Makes 6 to 8 servings

Special tools: 9 x 13-inch baking dish

GLUTEN-FREE (IF GLUTEN-FREE PASTA IS USED)
VEGETARIAN (IF VEGGIE BROTH IS USED)
NUT-FREE
FREEZER-FRIENDLY

1 tablespoon olive oil

1 small onion, finely diced

5 garlic cloves, minced

1 teaspoon Italian seasoning

Pinch of red pepper flakes, or more to taste

One 28-ounce can crushed tomatoes

1 cup chicken or veggie broth

Salt

16 ounces small whole wheat pasta shells, cooked al dente according to the package directions

One 15-ounce container ricotta cheese

8 ounces mozzarella cheese, grated (about 2 cups)

Suggested accompaniments: A big green salad and some warm Garlic Toast (page 141)

I don't think my eleven-year-old has ever met a noodle she didn't like, and this dish is no exception! This is a super-easy meal to throw together on a busy weeknight with lots of hands-off time while it's baking, and, bonus—it's filling even without any meat, which helps keep the cost down.

1. Preheat the oven to 425°F.

2. In a large skillet, heat the olive oil over medium heat. Add the onion and sauté until it begins to soften but not brown, 2 to 3 minutes. Add the garlic, Italian seasoning, and pepper flakes and cook, stirring constantly, for 1 minute.

3. Add the crushed tomatoes and broth, bring to a boil, and reduce the heat to low. Simmer until the sauce begins to thicken, about 10 minutes, and season with salt to taste and more pepper flakes, if desired.

4. Meanwhile, in a large bowl, combine the pasta, ricotta, and mozzarella and gently mix.

5. Pour half the sauce into a 9 x 13-inch baking dish. Spread the pasta and cheese mixture on top. Evenly pour the remaining sauce over the pasta.

6. Bake until golden brown around the edges and bubbling, 20 to 25 minutes.

SHOPPING LIST		TOTAL	$11.78
		COST PER SERVING	$1.47
One 16-ounce box whole wheat pasta shells	$1.69		
1 small onion	$0.56	**PANTRY AND FRIDGE CHECKLIST**	
1 garlic head	$0.50	1 tablespoon olive oil	
One 28-ounce can crushed tomatoes	$1.28	1 teaspoon Italian seasoning	
One 14.5-ounce can chicken or veggie broth	$1.37	Salt	
		Red pepper flakes	
One 15-ounce container ricotta cheese	$2.49	**INGREDIENTS LEFT OVER**	
One 8-ounce block mozzarella cheese	$3.89	Garlic	
		Broth	

LISA'S TIP: All my recipe testers unanimously said this one was a big hit with their little ones. One kid who normally hates lasagna asked for it again the next day!

I have some recipe splurge suggestions for this one if you're in the mood to treat yourself! In step 3, pour in ¼ cup red wine and let it almost completely boil off before pouring in the tomatoes and broth. And in step 5, sprinkle ½ cup grated Parmesan on top before baking it. I love a dish with different variations.

Fast-Food Chicken Nuggets

Difficulty: Medium
Prep time: 20 to 25 minutes
   (plus 1 hour to marinate)
Cook time: 14 to 16 minutes (if
   cooked in 2 batches)
Makes 5 or 6 servings
Special tools: Loaf pan or
   small baking dish and meat
   tenderizer

DAIRY-FREE
NUT-FREE
FREEZER-FRIENDLY

1½ pounds boneless, skinless
chicken breasts

1 cup pickle juice

2 eggs

1 cup whole wheat flour

2 teaspoons paprika

1 teaspoon garlic powder

1 teaspoon salt

½ teaspoon ground black
pepper

¼ teaspoon mustard powder

Olive oil, for cooking

"This was a hit! Any
time we have chicken
nuggets, I make them
homemade. But this
was my kids' favorite
nugget recipe by far."

—Summer Morrell,
recipe tester

I often make homemade breadcrumb-coated chicken nuggets (the recipe is in my first cookbook), but this version— marinated in pickle juice—is reminiscent of the fast-food nuggets sold at Chick-fil-A—although much better for you, of course! Inspired by my friend Carrie Vitt of Deliciously Organic, these nuggets never last long at my house.

1. Set the chicken on a cutting board, cover with a layer of plastic wrap to prevent splatters, and pound on both sides until evenly tenderized (I like to spend a little more time on the thicker sides of each piece).

2. Place the chicken in a loaf pan and pour in enough pickle juice to cover (about 1 cup). Cover with plastic wrap and refrigerate for at least 1 hour or up to 24 hours.

3. Remove the chicken (discard the pickle juice) and cut into 1½-inch chunks.

4. Lightly whisk the eggs in a shallow bowl. Toss the flour, paprika, garlic powder, salt, pepper, and mustard together on a plate.

5. Designate one hand as your "wet hand" (for the eggs) and one as your "dry hand" (for the flour mixture). With your wet hand, toss some of the chicken chunks into the egg mixture until they are coated on all sides, then drop them in the flour mixture. With your dry hand, sprinkle some flour on top of the chicken pieces and roll them around until evenly coated. Place the coated pieces on a clean plate while you coat the rest of the chicken.

6. In a large skillet, heat a thin layer of olive oil over medium heat. Working in batches, cook the chicken nuggets until golden brown and cooked all the way through (no longer pink), 3 to 4 minutes per side. Be careful not to overcrowd the pan.

7. Serve warm and freeze the leftovers for up to 6 months.

SHOPPING LIST

1½ pounds boneless, skinless chicken breasts	$5.24
One 16-ounce jar pickles	$1.99
Half dozen eggs	$0.85
One 2-pound bag whole wheat flour	$3.49
TOTAL	**$11.57**
COST PER SERVING	**$1.93**

PANTRY AND FRIDGE CHECKLIST

2 teaspoons paprika
1 teaspoon garlic powder
Salt and pepper
¼ teaspoon mustard powder
Olive oil, for cooking

INGREDIENTS LEFT OVER

Pickles
Eggs
Flour

Baked Bean–Stuffed Potatoes

Difficulty: Easy
Prep time: 10 to 15 minutes
Cook time: 15 to 20 minutes
Makes 4 servings

GLUTEN-FREE
DAIRY-FREE (IF OPTIONAL BUTTER IS OMITTED)
NUT-FREE

2 slices bacon

½ yellow onion, diced

One 15-ounce can navy beans, drained and rinsed

1 cup tomato sauce

¼ cup pure maple syrup

1 tablespoon yellow mustard

1 tablespoon apple cider vinegar

1 teaspoon chili powder

½ teaspoon salt

Cayenne pepper

2 large russet (baking) potatoes, baked (see Tip)

Butter (optional)

I'm a huge baked potato fan (the more toppings the better!) and the shortcut baked beans in this version practically turn this dish into a full meal. If you have any potato skin left when you are done, you can fry it in some butter in a skillet for a fabulous little leftover treat.

1. In a large skillet, cook the bacon over medium heat until crisp, 2 to 3 minutes per side. Drain the bacon on paper towels (leaving the grease in the pan) and crumble.

2. Still over medium heat, add the onion to the skillet and cook in the bacon grease until softened, 2 to 3 minutes.

3. Add the beans, tomato sauce, maple syrup, mustard, vinegar, chili powder, salt, and cayenne to taste. Toss in the bacon and stir to combine. Bring to a boil, reduce the heat to low, and simmer until the sauce thickens, 15 to 20 minutes.

4. Halve the baked potatoes lengthwise, break up the flesh with the back of a fork, and spread a little butter on top (if desired). Evenly divide the bean mixture over the potatoes and serve warm.

SHOPPING LIST		PANTRY AND FRIDGE CHECKLIST
2 russet (baking) potatoes (about 8 ounces each)	$1.29	¼ cup pure maple syrup
One 8-ounce package bacon	$4.19	1 tablespoon yellow mustard
1 onion (8 ounces)	$0.85	1 tablespoon apple cider vinegar
One 15-ounce can navy beans	$0.91	1 teaspoon chili powder
One 8-ounce can tomato sauce	$0.27	Salt
		Cayenne pepper
TOTAL	**$7.51**	**INGREDIENTS LEFT OVER**
COST PER SERVING	**$1.50**	Bacon

LISA'S TIP: Baked potatoes *can* be made in the microwave, but I honestly think they turn out better (and are more evenly cooked) in the oven. Plus, as long as you have enough time, it's simple, really. Preheat the oven to 425°F. Scrub the potatoes clean, prick a few holes in the skin with a fork, and bake until tender when pierced with a fork, 45 to 55 minutes.

Creamy Braised Pork Chops

If you've got a weakness for delicious sauces (like me), then you'll love this braised pork recipe! My family was scraping every last bit of this sauce from the pan and pouring whatever they could spare over their mashed potatoes (page 132). And the pork in this recipe could easily be replaced with chicken if you desire. Just increase the cooking time, since a chicken breast is likely to be thicker than a thin pork chop.

1. In a small bowl, mix the paprika, onion powder, garlic powder, salt, and pepper. Sprinkle over both sides of the pork chops until evenly coated.

2. In a large skillet, melt 2 tablespoons of the butter over medium heat. Sear the pork chops until golden brown on both sides, 1 to 2 minutes per side.

3. Add the cream and the remaining 2 tablespoons butter, reduce the heat to low, and cover with a tight-fitting lid. Cook until the pork is no longer pink in the middle, 3 to 4 minutes. Uncover and cook to let the sauce thicken for another minute.

Difficulty: Easy
Prep time: 10 to 15 minutes
Cook time: 6 to 8 minutes
Makes 4 servings
Special tools: Small jar with tight-fitting lid

GLUTEN-FREE
NUT-FREE

1 teaspoon paprika

1 teaspoon onion powder

1 teaspoon garlic powder

½ teaspoon salt

¼ teaspoon ground black pepper

1¼ pounds thin boneless pork chops

4 tablespoons (½ stick) butter

1 cup heavy cream

SHOPPING LIST		PANTRY AND FRIDGE CHECKLIST
1¼ pounds thin boneless pork chops	$6.61	1 teaspoon paprika
½ pint heavy cream	$2.29	1 teaspoon onion powder
TOTAL	**$8.90**	1 teaspoon garlic powder
COST PER SERVING	**$2.23**	Salt and pepper
		4 tablespoons (½ stick) butter

INGREDIENTS LEFT OVER
N/A

Cheesy Eggplant Bake

Difficulty: Easy

Prep time: 15 minutes

Cook time: 30 to 35 minutes (mostly hands-off)

Makes 6 servings

Special tools: 9 x 13-inch baking dish

GLUTEN-FREE
VEGETARIAN
NUT-FREE
FREEZER-FRIENDLY

3 tablespoons olive oil

1 large eggplant (about 2 pounds), cut into 1-inch cubes

Salt and ground black pepper

3 cups marinara sauce

6 ounces mozzarella cheese, shredded

¼ cup freshly grated Parmesan cheese

Suggested accompaniments: Cooked whole grain pasta and fresh basil leaves

Eggplant is not my kids' most favorite vegetable by itself, so I really have to cover it up with other yummy flavors for it to be a hit at the dinner table. We love this dish served over whole-grain pasta for an easy and filling meatless meal.

1. Preheat the oven to 375°F.

2. In your largest skillet, heat the olive oil over medium heat. Add the eggplant and cook, stirring occasionally, until it darkens in color, 5 to 8 minutes. Season with salt and pepper.

3. Pour half the marinara sauce into a 9 x 13-inch inch baking dish. Shake it around to ensure it's evenly spread. Sprinkle the eggplant cubes evenly over the sauce.

4. Sprinkle all but ½ cup of the mozzarella over the eggplant, pour in the rest of the sauce, and top with the remaining mozzarella and the Parmesan.

5. Bake until bubbling and golden brown, 25 to 30 minutes. If desired, serve warm over whole wheat pasta and topped with fresh basil.

SHOPPING LIST	
1 large eggplant (2 pounds)	$3.98
Two 24-ounce jars marinara sauce	$3.26
One 8-ounce block mozzarella cheese	$3.89
One 6-ounce tub freshly grated Parmesan cheese	$3.99
TOTAL	**$15.12**
COST PER SERVING	**$2.52**

PANTRY AND FRIDGE CHECKLIST

3 tablespoons olive oil
Salt and pepper

INGREDIENTS LEFT OVER

Marinara sauce
Mozzarella
Parmesan cheese

Sienna's Chicken and Sweet Potato Quesadillas

Difficulty: Easy
Prep time: 20 minutes
Cook time: 20 to 30 minutes
Makes 5 or 6 servings
Special tools: Potato masher

GLUTEN-FREE
NUT-FREE
FREEZER-FRIENDLY

1 tablespoon olive oil

1 pound boneless, skinless chicken thighs, cut into 1-inch pieces

4 ounces sweet potato (about ½ small), unpeeled, cut into ½-inch dice

½ green bell pepper, cored, seeded, and diced

½ yellow onion, minced

1½ teaspoons ground cumin

½ teaspoon garlic powder

½ teaspoon cayenne pepper

½ teaspoon salt

One 8-ounce block Monterey Jack cheese, shredded (2 to 2½ cups)

12 whole-grain corn tortillas

Butter, for frying

Suggested accompaniments: Sour cream and lime wedges

This is the meal my younger daughter made when I put her in charge of dinner on one night of our vacation (as mentioned on page 175). She was so excited that she started asking me at two that afternoon if she could start working on it! Amazing things can happen when you empower your kids in the kitchen, and no matter how old they are, it's never too late to start.

1.   In a large skillet, heat the olive oil over medium heat. Add the chicken and sweet potato and cook, stirring occasionally, until the chicken starts to brown, 4 to 5 minutes.

2.   Add the bell pepper, onion, cumin, garlic powder, cayenne, and salt and cook until the sweet potatoes are tender when pierced with a fork and the chicken is cooked all the way through (no longer pink), 5 to 6 minutes. Use a potato masher to smooth out the mixture and reduce the large chunks.

3.   Lay out 6 tortillas and evenly distribute the cheese and chicken filling on them. Top with the remaining tortillas.

4.   Wipe out the skillet and place it over medium heat (or set an electric griddle to 350°F). Melt a pat of butter in the pan. Working in batches, place the quesadillas in the pan. Mash them down with the spatula to help them stick together. Smear another small pat of butter on each top tortilla to help grease the pan when you flip the quesadillas over. Cook until the tortillas are golden brown, 3 to 5 minutes on each side. Transfer the first batch of quesadillas to a large cutting board to cool while you cook the remaining quesadillas.

5.   When the cheese is slightly cooled and set, cut each quesadilla into 4 slices. A pizza cutter makes this job easy.

6.   Garnish with sour cream and lime wedges, if desired, and serve.

SHOPPING LIST

1 pound boneless,
  skinless chicken thighs $2.69
1 small sweet potato
  (8 ounces) $0.65
1 yellow onion $0.56
1 green bell pepper $0.99
One 8-ounce block
  Monterey Jack cheese $3.89

Two 8-count packages
  whole-grain corn tortillas $3.78

TOTAL   **$12.56**
COST PER SERVING   **$2.09**

PANTRY AND FRIDGE CHECKLIST

1 tablespoon olive oil
1½ teaspoons ground cumin
½ teaspoon cayenne pepper

½ teaspoon garlic powder
Salt
Butter, for frying

INGREDIENTS LEFT OVER

Sweet potato
Onion
Green bell pepper
Tortillas

Spaghetti Squash Carbonara

Difficulty: Medium
Prep time: 15 minutes
Cook time: 45 to 55 minutes
(mostly hands-off)
Makes 4 servings
Special tools: Large baking
sheet

GLUTEN-FREE
NUT-FREE
FREEZER-FRIENDLY

Oil, for the pan
1 spaghetti squash (about
2¼ pounds)
One 8-ounce package bacon
2 eggs
½ cup freshly grated Parmesan
cheese
½ onion, diced
1 garlic clove, minced
Salt and ground black pepper

Suggested accompaniment:
Parsley

One of the things I love about eating spaghetti squash is that my mental veggie consumption checklist for my family goes . . . check, check, and check! And it tastes great too—especially in this recipe; my eleven-year-old isn't a huge fan when I pair spaghetti squash with marinara sauce, but she'll scarf down just about anything that is creamy and includes bacon (hard to blame her!). I hope this one is a hit at your house as well.

1. Preheat the oven to 400°F. Oil a large baking sheet.

2. Cut the squash in half lengthwise and scoop out (and discard) the seeds. Place it flesh side down on the baking sheet and bake until tender when pierced with a fork, 40 to 50 minutes. Use a fork to shred the squash into noodle-like strands.

3. Meanwhile, in a large skillet, cook the bacon over medium heat until browned on both sides and crispy, 3 to 4 minutes per side. Transfer the bacon to paper towels to drain and crumble. Pour all but 1 tablespoon of the bacon grease out of the pan.

4. In a medium bowl, whisk the eggs and Parmesan. Set aside.

5. Cook the onion and garlic in the bacon grease over medium heat until the onion begins to soften, 3 to 5 minutes. Add the squash "noodles" and remove from the heat.

6. While stirring constantly, pour in the egg mixture. Return the pan to medium-low heat and stir constantly just until the sauce thickens, 4 to 5 minutes. It's better to have a tired arm than curdled eggs!

7. Transfer to a serving dish, mix in the crumbled bacon, and serve warm.

SHOPPING LIST

1 spaghetti squash
  (2¼ pounds) $4.48
One 8-ounce package
  bacon $4.19
1 small onion $0.56
1 garlic head $0.50
Half dozen eggs $0.85

One 6-ounce tub freshly
  grated Parmesan cheese $3.99
TOTAL   **$14.57**
COST PER SERVING   **$3.64**

**PANTRY AND FRIDGE
CHECKLIST**

Salt and pepper
Oil, for greasing

INGREDIENTS LEFT OVER

Onion
Garlic
Eggs
Parmesan cheese

Teriyaki Beef Skewers

There's just something fun about food on a stick—kids especially love it! And marinating and thinly slicing makes this budget-friendly cut of meat tender and tasty. Serve this crowd-pleasing dish with brown rice and a green veggie for a simple weeknight meal.

1. If using wooden skewers, soak them in water for a minimum of 30 minutes to keep them from burning in the oven.

2. To make the marinade, in a medium bowl, whisk together the soy sauce, water, vinegar, sesame oil, honey, and ginger.

3. Cut the steak against the grain into ¼- to ½-inch-thick slices. Add the beef to the marinade so it's completely submerged. Cover and refrigerate for at least 1 hour or as long as overnight.

4. Position a rack about 4 inches from the broiler element and turn the broiler to high. Thread the meat onto the skewers and place them on the prepared baking sheet. Broil for 2 to 3 minutes, turn the skewers over, and broil until the meat is a crispy brown on the edges and no longer pink in the middle, 2 to 4 minutes longer. Serve warm on the skewers.

Difficulty: Super easy
Prep time: 15 minutes (plus an hour to marinate)
Cook time: 5 to 6 minutes
Makes 4 servings
Special tools: 12 metal or wooden skewers and a baking sheet lined with foil

GLUTEN-FREE (IF GLUTEN-FREE SOY SAUCE IS USED)
DAIRY-FREE
NUT-FREE
FREEZER-FRIENDLY

⅓ cup soy sauce
⅓ cup water
1 tablespoon rice vinegar
1 tablespoon toasted sesame oil
1 tablespoon honey
2 teaspoons grated fresh ginger
1 pound flank steak

SHOPPING LIST		PANTRY AND FRIDGE CHECKLIST
One 15-ounce bottle soy sauce	$2.49	1 tablespoon rice vinegar
2 ounces fresh ginger	$0.63	1 tablespoon toasted sesame oil
1 pound flank steak	$6.99	1 tablespoon honey
TOTAL	**$10.11**	**INGREDIENTS LEFT OVER**
COST PER SERVING		Soy sauce
(3 skewers)	**$2.53**	

LISA'S TIP: These skewers could also be thrown on the outdoor grill!

Easy Chicken Scaloppine

Difficulty: Medium
Prep time: 15 minutes
Cook time: 10 minutes
Makes 3 or 4 servings
Special tools: Meat tenderizer

DAIRY-FREE
NUT-FREE
FREEZER-FRIENDLY

1 pound boneless, skinless chicken breasts

½ cup whole wheat flour

1 teaspoon garlic powder/ granules

1 teaspoon onion powder

2 to 3 tablespoons olive oil

Juice of 1 lemon

Salt and ground black pepper

Suggested accompaniments: Cooked whole-grain noodles or rice and your favorite vegetable

The first time I made this my thirteen-year-old said, "How did you make this chicken so good?" I tenderized (pounded) it, I told her. She asked me to always pound the chicken from now on! She's not always the biggest meat eater, but she's a fan when the chicken is super tender. I'll have to add that note to my running mental list of my children's likes and dislikes (which seem to change day to day).

1. Place the chicken on a cutting board with a layer of plastic wrap on top (to prevent splatters). Pound the chicken on both sides until evenly tenderized. I like to spend a little more time on the thicker sides of each piece.

2. On a plate, mix the flour, garlic powder, and onion powder with a fork. Dredge the chicken in the mixture until evenly coated.

3. In a large skillet, heat 2 tablespoons olive oil over medium-high heat. Cook the chicken until golden brown on both sides and cooked all the way through (no longer pink in the middle), 4 to 5 minutes per side. If the pan gets dry, add the additional tablespoon of olive oil.

4. Sprinkle the lemon juice on top, season with salt and pepper, and serve warm.

SHOPPING LIST		PANTRY AND FRIDGE CHECKLIST
1 pound boneless, skinless chicken breasts	$3.49	1 teaspoon garlic powder
One 2-pound bag whole wheat flour	$3.49	1 teaspoon onion powder
1 lemon	$0.65	Salt and pepper
		2 to 3 tablespoons olive oil
TOTAL	**$7.63**	**INGREDIENTS LEFT OVER**
COST PER SERVING	**$1.91**	Whole wheat flour

Quick and Easy Fried Rice

Frozen, precut, mixed veggies not only save money but time! Not having to wash, peel, and chop (and even select) all the different fresh veggies in this meal is a welcome time saver, without sacrificing too much in the way of taste. When there are a lot of flavors going on, as in this fried rice recipe, I find it harder to detect the difference between fresh and frozen.

1. In a large sauté pan or wok, heat the oil over medium-high heat. Add the onion and ginger and cook, stirring constantly, until just beginning to soften, 1 to 2 minutes. Stir in the garlic and cook for another 30 seconds or so.

2. Pour the frozen veggies into the pan and cook, stirring often, until heated through, 3 to 4 minutes.

3. Using a spatula, push the veggie mixture to one side of the pan. Drop in the 2 eggs on the other side and cook while scrambling for 1 to 2 minutes, then stir the entire mixture together. Season with salt and cayenne or black pepper to taste.

4. When the eggs are fully cooked, add the soy sauce, sesame oil, and rice. Mix thoroughly until everything is heated and serve warm.

Difficulty: Easy
Prep time: 15 minutes
Cook time: 10 to 12 minutes
Makes 4 servings

GLUTEN-FREE (IF GLUTEN-FREE SOY SAUCE IS USED)
DAIRY-FREE
VEGETARIAN
NUT-FREE

1 tablespoon olive oil or coconut oil

½ cup diced onion

1 teaspoon minced fresh ginger

2 garlic cloves, minced

One 10-ounce bag chopped mixed frozen veggies (I like a stir-fry blend or Chinese-style for this recipe), no need to thaw

2 eggs

Salt

Cayenne or ground black pepper

¼ cup soy sauce, preferably reduced-sodium

½ teaspoon toasted sesame oil

1 cup brown rice, cooked according to package directions

SHOPPING LIST		PANTRY AND FRIDGE CHECKLIST
One 16-ounce bag brown rice	$1.00	1 tablespoon olive oil or coconut oil
1 yellow onion	$0.85	¼ cup soy sauce
1 garlic head	$0.50	½ teaspoon toasted sesame oil
2 ounces fresh ginger	$0.63	Salt and pepper
One 10-ounce bag mixed frozen veggies (stir-fry blend or Chinese-style)	$1.69	**INGREDIENTS LEFT OVER**
Half dozen eggs	$0.85	Brown rice
TOTAL	**$5.52**	Onion
COST PER SERVING	**$1.38**	Garlic
		Eggs

Swedish Meatballs

Difficulty: Medium
Prep time: 15 to 20 minutes
Cook time: 13 to 17 minutes
Makes 4 servings

NUT-FREE
FREEZER-FRIENDLY

MEATBALLS

1 tablespoon butter or olive oil

½ cup minced onion

½ pound ground beef

½ pound ground pork

¼ cup whole wheat breadcrumbs

¼ cup heavy cream

½ teaspoon salt, plus more to taste

¼ teaspoon ground black pepper, plus more to taste

Pinch of ground allspice

SAUCE AND ACCOMPANIMENTS

5 large carrots, peeled and cut into 1-inch chunks

2 tablespoons whole wheat flour

1½ cups beef, chicken, or veggie broth

½ cup heavy cream

½ teaspoon soy sauce

Salt and ground black pepper

Cooked whole wheat egg noodles, 4 servings

All it took was a couple of trips to Ikea for me to crave some good ol' Swedish meatballs. Now, I don't think I've ever met a meatball I didn't like, and these are a nice change of pace from the usual Italian. My family devoured this one-dish dinner, and it even had my eleven-year-old asking for thirds. Yes, thirds! So be smart and double the recipe if you're counting on leftovers for lunch.

1. To make the meatballs: In a large sauté pan (big enough to fit all the meatballs and carrots later), melt the butter over medium heat. Add the onion and cook, stirring occasionally, until it begins to soften, 2 to 3 minutes.

2. Dump the onion into a large bowl along with the beef, pork, breadcrumbs, heavy cream, ½ teaspoon salt, ¼ teaspoon pepper, and allspice. Mix well by hand and form into roughly sixteen 1½-inch meatballs.

3. To cook the meatballs and make the sauce: Return the pan to medium-high heat, add the meatballs and carrots (and more butter if necessary), and cook until the meatballs are browned and almost crispy on all sides, 5 to 6 minutes. (You can cook the carrots in a separate skillet with additional butter if your pan feels too small to hold it all.)

4. Sprinkle the flour on top and cook, stirring, for a minute or so to let it absorb. Add the broth, cream, and soy sauce and bring to a boil, scraping the browned bits off the bottom of the pan. Simmer until the sauce thickens to a gravy, the meatballs are cooked all the way through, and the carrots are tender when pierced with a fork, 6 to 8 minutes.

5. Season with salt and pepper, spoon over whole wheat egg noodles, and serve.

SHOPPING LIST

1 small onion	$0.56
½ pound ground beef	$2.00
½ pound ground pork	$1.25
One 15-ounce canister whole wheat breadcrumbs	$2.89
½ pint heavy cream	$2.29
One 1-pound bag carrots	$0.99
One 12-ounce bag whole wheat egg noodles	$2.39
One 14.5-ounce can broth (chicken, veggie, or beef)	$1.37
TOTAL	**$13.74**
COST PER SERVING (4 meatballs)	**$3.44**

PANTRY AND FRIDGE CHECKLIST

1 tablespoon butter or olive oil
Pinch of ground allspice
2 tablespoons whole wheat flour
½ teaspoon soy sauce
Salt and pepper

INGREDIENTS LEFT OVER

Onion
Breadcrumbs
Heavy cream
Broth

Baked Sweet Potato Taquitos

The first time I made taquitos, my kids went a little nuts with excitement and didn't hesitate to help themselves to an extra-large portion! So if you get the same reaction at your house, you'll be glad this recipe makes so many taquitos. Nothing wrong with loading the kids up with veggies, beans, and whole grains.

1. Preheat the oven to 425°F. Line a 13 x 18-inch baking sheet with parchment paper.

2. Using a food processor with a shredding disk, grate the unpeeled potato into small shreds (or use a hand grater).

3. In a large skillet, heat the oil over medium heat. Stir in the sweet potato and cook until it begins to turn golden brown, about 5 minutes, stirring occasionally. Add water, cover the pan, and steam until the potatoes are tender, 2 to 3 minutes. Uncover and stir in the beans, corn, cumin, salt, and Monterey Jack. Remove from the heat.

4. Warm the tortillas by wrapping them in a damp paper towel and heating them for 30 seconds or so in the microwave. Add a spoonful of filling to a tortilla, carefully roll it up, and place it seam side down on the baking sheet. Repeat to make the rest of the taquitos.

5. Bake until the taquitos are golden brown and crisp on the edges, 15 to 20 minutes. Serve warm with sour cream and cilantro.

Difficulty: Medium
Prep time: 15 to 20 minutes
Cook time: Less than 30 minutes
Makes 20 to 22 taquitos / 5 or 6 servings
Special tools: Large skillet with a tight-fitting lid, 13 x 18-inch baking sheet lined with parchment paper, and food processor (not necessary, but helpful)

GLUTEN-FREE
VEGETARIAN
NUT-FREE
FREEZER-FRIENDLY

1 small to medium sweet potato (8 to 12 ounces), unpeeled

2 tablespoons olive oil

½ cup water

One 15-ounce can black beans, drained and rinsed

1 cup frozen corn kernels (no need to thaw)

1 teaspoon ground cumin

½ teaspoon salt

1 cup (about 5 ounces) shredded Monterey Jack cheese

20 to 22 whole-grain corn tortillas

For serving:
Sour cream and cilantro

SHOPPING LIST		
1 small to medium sweet potato (8 to 12 ounces)	$0.65	
One 15-ounce can black beans	$0.95	
One 15-ounce bag frozen corn kernels	$1.69	
One 8-ounce block Monterey Jack cheese	$3.89	
Three 8-count packages whole-grain corn tortillas	$5.67	
One 8-ounce container sour cream	$0.99	

TOTAL	**$13.84**
COST PER SERVING	**$2.30**

PANTRY AND FRIDGE CHECKLIST
2 tablespoons olive oil
1 teaspoon ground cumin
Salt

INGREDIENTS LEFT OVER
Corn
Monterey Jack cheese
Tortillas

Weeknight Tandoori Chicken

Difficulty: Easy
Prep time: 10 to 15 minutes
Cook time: 12 to 16 minutes
Makes 6 servings

GLUTEN-FREE
**DAIRY-FREE (IF YOGURT
 ACCOMPANIMENT IS NOT USED)**
**FREEZER-FRIENDLY (WITHOUT
ACCOMPANIMENTS)**
NUT-FREE

1½ teaspoons garlic powder

1½ teaspoons ground coriander

1½ teaspoons ground cumin

1 teaspoon ground ginger

1 teaspoon salt

½ teaspoon cayenne pepper

1½ pounds boneless, skinless
chicken thighs

1 tablespoon olive oil or
coconut oil

One 13-ounce can coconut milk

One 8-ounce can tomato sauce

2 ounces fresh spinach (2 to
2½ cups)

6 servings brown rice,
cooked according to package
directions

Suggested accompaniments:
Cilantro, mint leaves, and plain
yogurt

I almost never think to cook Indian food for some reason, but we received tandoori chicken in a Blue Apron box once and it turned out to be really good (love how those boxes help us branch out on occasion)! So I decided to make my own version of this flavorful recipe, and it's quick and easy enough for any busy weeknight.

1. In a medium bowl, combine the garlic powder, coriander, cumin, ginger, salt, and cayenne with a fork. Dredge the chicken in the spice mixture and set aside.

2. In a large skillet, heat the oil over medium heat. Add the chicken, sprinkle any remaining spices on top, and sear until golden brown, 2 to 3 minutes on each side.

3. Add the coconut milk and tomato sauce, bring to a boil, and cover with a lid. Reduce the heat to low and cook until the chicken is done all the way through (no longer pink), 8 to 10 minutes.

4. Layer in bowls with brown rice on the bottom, then spinach, chicken, sauce, yogurt, and fresh herbs. Enjoy!

SHOPPING LIST	
1½ pounds boneless, skinless chicken thighs	$4.04
One 13.5-ounce can coconut milk	$1.49
One 8-ounce can tomato sauce	$0.27
One 5-ounce bag fresh spinach	$2.49
One 16-ounce bag brown rice	$1.00
TOTAL	**$9.29**
COST PER SERVING	**$1.55**

PANTRY AND FRIDGE CHECKLIST

1½ teaspoons garlic powder
1½ teaspoons ground coriander
1½ teaspoons ground cumin
1 teaspoon ground ginger
Salt
½ teaspoon cayenne pepper
1 tablespoon olive oil or coconut oil

INGREDIENTS LEFT OVER

Spinach
Brown rice

SHOPPING LIST

Two 8-count packages whole-grain corn tortillas	$3.78
1 small onion	$0.56
1 zucchini	$1.27
One 15-ounce can black beans	$0.95
One 15-ounce bag frozen corn kernels	$1.69
One 8-ounce container sour cream	$0.99
Two 15-ounce cans tomato sauce	$2.26
One 8-ounce block Monterey Jack cheese	$3.89
TOTAL	**$15.39**
COST PER SERVING (3 enchiladas)	**$3.85**

PANTRY AND FRIDGE CHECKLIST

1 tablespoon olive oil
1 tablespoon chili powder
2 teaspoons ground cumin
1/4 teaspoon cayenne pepper
Salt
Cilantro (garden)

INGREDIENTS LEFT OVER

Tortillas
Onion
Corn
Sour cream

Zucchini and Black Bean Enchiladas

If you grow your own veggies in the summer, you may know a little something about needing to get creative with zucchini. This was my answer one year when I was lucky enough to have a plant doing well. The zucchini and black beans together in this dish turned out to be a great combination.

1. Preheat the oven to 400°F.

2. In a large skillet, heat the oil over medium-high heat. Add the onion and zucchini and cook, stirring occasionally, until they begin to soften, 4 to 5 minutes. Add the beans and corn and cook until heated through, 1 to 2 minutes. Remove from the heat.

3. In a small saucepan, whisk the tomato sauce, chili powder, cumin, salt, and cayenne and cook over low heat until heated through. Set aside and keep the sauce warm until needed.

4. Warm the tortillas by wrapping them in a damp paper towel and heating them for 30 seconds or so in the microwave.

5. Spread half the sauce onto the bottom of a 9 x 13-inch baking dish. Scoop a spoonful of the filling onto a tortilla, along with a tablespoon of Monterey Jack, and roll up the tortilla. Place it seam side down on the sauce in the dish. Repeat to make the rest of the enchiladas. Top with any remaining veggies and cheese and completely cover the enchiladas with the remaining sauce.

6. Bake until the cheese on top is golden brown, 20 to 25 minutes. Serve warm topped with sour cream and cilantro.

Difficulty: Medium
Prep time: 15 minutes
Cook time: About 30 minutes (mostly hands-off)
Makes 4 servings
Special tools: 9 x 13-inch baking dish

GLUTEN-FREE
VEGETARIAN
NUT-FREE
FREEZER-FRIENDLY

1 tablespoon olive oil

½ small yellow onion, thinly sliced

1 zucchini, trimmed, halved crosswise, and cut into ½-inch-thick strips

One 15-ounce can black beans, drained and rinsed

1 cup frozen corn kernels (no need to thaw)

Two 15-ounce cans tomato sauce

1 tablespoon chili powder

2 teaspoons ground cumin

1 teaspoon salt

¼ teaspoon cayenne pepper, or more to taste

12 whole-grain corn tortillas

2 cups grated Monterey Jack cheese

For serving: Sour cream and cilantro

Breadcrumb-Roasted Chicken

Difficulty: Easy
Prep time: 10 to 15 minutes
Cook time: 25 to 30 minutes (hands-off)
Makes 4 or 5 servings
Special tools: 8- or 9-inch square (or round or oval) baking dish

NUT-FREE
FREEZER-FRIENDLY

1½ pounds boneless, skinless chicken breasts

Salt and ground black pepper

1 cup whole wheat panko-style breadcrumbs (see Tip)

2 tablespoons fresh thyme leaves

2 tablespoons chopped fresh parsley

Grated zest of 1 lemon

4 tablespoons (½ stick) butter, melted

One of our favorite holiday dinners is roasted rack of lamb with a yummy bread-crumb, herb, and olive oil mixture on top (from a favorite Australian cookbook by Bill Granger that I've had forever). Now, we're not ones to eat rack of lamb every week—not to mention that would totally break the budget!—so I was inspired to try a similar breadcrumb mixture on top of a cut of meat that's more everyday: chicken breasts. This is tasty as a main dish or great left over served on top of a salad or some pasta, too.

1. Preheat the oven to 375°F.

2. Cut the chicken into slices 1½ to 2 inches thick (tenders). Place in a baking dish and season with salt and pepper.

3. In a small bowl, combine the breadcrumbs, thyme, parsley, and lemon zest. Stir in the melted butter and spread the mixture over the chicken.

4. Bake until golden brown on top and the chicken is done (no longer pink) in the thickest part, 25 to 30 minutes. Serve warm.

SHOPPING LIST		PANTRY AND FRIDGE CHECKLIST
1½ pounds boneless, skinless chicken breasts	$5.24	Salt and pepper
One 15-ounce canister whole wheat breadcrumbs	$2.89	Thyme (garden)
1 lemon	$0.65	Parsley (garden)
TOTAL	**$8.78**	4 tablespoons (½ stick) butter
COST PER SERVING	**$1.76**	**INGREDIENTS LEFT OVER**
		Breadcrumbs
		Lemon (save for juicing)

LISA'S TIPS: Herbs: If you want to sub dried herbs for fresh, use 1 teaspoon dried per 1 tablespoon fresh. Breadcrumbs: Homemade breadcrumbs are easy to make! Simply preheat the oven to 300°F, grind up 6 pieces of dried-out whole wheat bread in a food processor, spread the crumbs on a baking sheet, and bake until golden brown, 20 to 25 minutes, stirring a couple of times.

slow cooker favorites

slow cooker favorite recipes

Slow Cooker Cuban Pork

Cuban food is not something we think to make often, but if you haven't tried it and enjoy different foods and flavors, this is a great recipe to throw in the mix. And if you have some bread, cheese, and pickles on hand, you can turn the leftovers into a tasty sandwich for lunch the next day.

1. Place the onion in the slow cooker and set the pork on top. Combine the seasonings in a bowl and coat the meat on all sides with the spice mixture. Cover and cook on low for 7 to 8 hours, until the meat is tender and can be easily shredded with a fork.

2. Drain the meat and transfer to a serving bowl. Shred it with two forks, mix in the lime and orange juices, and, serve on a plate with side items of choice or sandwich style.

SHOPPING LIST		PANTRY AND FRIDGE CHECKLIST
3½ pounds pork shoulder	$11.52	2 teaspoons ground cumin
1 onion	$0.85	2 teaspoons dried oregano
1 lime	$0.25	1 teaspoon garlic powder
1 orange	$1.49	Salt and pepper
TOTAL	**$14.11**	
COST PER SERVING	**$2.35**	**INGREDIENTS LEFT OVER**
		N/A

Difficulty: Super easy
Prep time: 10 minutes
Cook time: 7 to 8 hours on low
Makes 6 servings by itself
    with sides or 8 servings as a
    sandwich
Special tools: Slow cooker

GLUTEN-FREE (WITHOUT SANDWICH FIXINGS)
DAIRY-FREE (WITHOUT SANDWICH FIXINGS)
NUT-FREE
FREEZER-FRIENDLY

1 onion, peeled and quartered
3½-pound pork shoulder roast
2 teaspoons salt
2 teaspoons ground cumin
2 teaspoons dried oregano
1 teaspoon garlic powder
½ teaspoon ground black pepper
Juice of 1 lime
Juice of 1 orange

Suggested accompaniments for sandwiches: Sliced cheese, pickles, and bread

Slow Cooker Mongolian Beef

Difficulty: Super easy
Prep time: 10 minutes
Cook time: 5 to 6 hours on high
Makes 5 or 6 servings
Special tools: Slow cooker

**GLUTEN-FREE (IF GLUTEN-FREE SOY
SAUCE IS USED)**
DAIRY-FREE
NUT-FREE
FREEZER-FRIENDLY

1¾ to 2 pounds stew beef
(budget option) or flank steak
(pricier option)

½ cup soy sauce

½ cup water

⅓ cup honey

2 garlic cloves, minced

1 teaspoon minced fresh ginger

Suggested accompaniments:
Sliced green onions, cooked
brown rice, and a green veggie
(such as Stir-Fry Broccoli, page
129)

This recipe will rival P. F. Chang's yummy dish, but it will be better for you! Most big chain restaurants don't cook from scratch (our preference) and use ingredients I wouldn't cook with at home, but no one has to miss out with this copycat dish that's super quick and easy to make.

1. Place the stew beef in the slow cooker. In a medium bowl, whisk together the soy sauce, water, honey, garlic, and ginger and pour over the meat.

2. Cover and cook on high for 5 to 6 hours, until tender enough to be easily shredded with a fork. Garnish with green onions and serve over brown rice with a green veggie on the side (if desired).

SHOPPING LIST		PANTRY AND FRIDGE CHECKLIST
1¾ pounds stew beef (or flank steak, for more money)	$9.47	N/A
One 15-ounce bottle soy sauce	$2.49	**INGREDIENTS LEFT OVER**
One 12-ounce jar honey	$2.50	Soy sauce
1 garlic head	$0.50	Honey
2 ounces fresh ginger	$0.63	Garlic
TOTAL	**$15.59**	Ginger
COST PER SERVING	**$2.60**	

Slow Cooker Carrot Curry Soup

Yellow curry is a flavor my whole family enjoys, but I often forget about it and go months without serving it. This recipe is a good reminder that vegetable soups don't have to be boring . . . or difficult to make, thanks to the slow cooker!

1. Combine all the ingredients except the garnish in a slow cooker. Cover and cook on high for 4 hours or on low for 6 to 7 hours, until the carrots are tender. Blend until smooth with an immersion blender (or in a stand blender in batches).

2. Serve warm, garnished with plain yogurt and cilantro.

Difficulty: Super easy
Prep time: 15 minutes
Cook time: 4 hours on high or
   6 to 7 hours on low
Makes 8 servings
Special tools: Slow cooker and
   blender (immersion or stand)

GLUTEN-FREE
**DAIRY-FREE (IF YOGURT GARNISH
   IS OMITTED)**
**VEGETARIAN (IF VEGETABLE BROTH
   IS USED)**
FREEZER-FRIENDLY

1 pound carrots, trimmed, peeled, and roughly chopped

½ yellow onion, diced

1 russet (baking) potato, unpeeled, cut into 1-inch pieces

One 13.5-ounce can coconut milk

2 cups vegetable or chicken broth

1 tablespoon curry powder

1 teaspoon ground cumin

1 teaspoon salt

Plain yogurt and fresh cilantro, for garnish

SHOPPING LIST		PANTRY AND FRIDGE CHECKLIST
1 pound carrots	$0.99	1 tablespoon curry powder
1 onion	$0.85	1 teaspoon ground cumin
1 potato	$0.65	Salt
One 13.5-ounce can coconut milk	$1.49	Cilantro (garden)
One 32-ounce container vegetable or chicken broth	$2.09	**INGREDIENTS LEFT OVER**
One 5.3-ounce container plain yogurt	$1.00	Onion
		Broth
TOTAL	**$7.07**	
COST PER SERVING	**$0.88**	

Slow Cooker Pulled Chicken Tacos

Difficulty: Super easy
Prep time: 10 minutes
Cook time: 4 hours on high or
    7 hours on low
Makes 6 to 8 servings
Special tools: Slow cooker

GLUTEN-FREE
**DAIRY-FREE (IF SOUR CREAM IS
    OMITTED)**
NUT-FREE
FREEZER-FRIENDLY

1 tablespoon chili powder
1 tablespoon ground cumin
1 tablespoon dried oregano
1 teaspoon salt
½ teaspoon ground black
pepper
1 onion, halved
1 whole chicken (about
4 pounds)
Juice of 1 lime

For serving: whole-grain corn
tortillas, sliced red cabbage,
sour cream, and cilantro

LISA'S TIP: This taco meat
is also tasty served over
brown rice instead of a tortilla!

If you're looking for a budget-friendly cut of meat, a whole chicken is the way to go. It's almost always cheaper (per pound) than any other cut. There's a little more work picking all the good meat off the bone, but you get much more bang for your buck. And I honestly like the taste better, too.

1. In a small bowl, combine the chili powder, cumin, oregano, salt, and pepper.

2. Place the onion in the slow cooker.

3. Remove any giblets from the chicken, then rub the spice mixture all over the outside of the chicken. Put the chicken breast side down on top of the onion and cover the slow cooker. There's no need to add any liquid.

4. Cook on high for 4 hours or on low for 7 hours, until the chicken is falling off the bone. Pick out the edible chicken pieces, shred the meat with a fork, drizzle a few spoonfuls of the cooking liquid (from the bottom of the slow cooker) on top, mix in the lime juice, and serve with the suggested taco fixings.

SHOPPING LIST		PANTRY AND FRIDGE CHECKLIST
1 onion	$0.85	1 tablespoon chili powder
1 whole chicken (4 pounds)	$5.16	1 tablespoon ground cumin
1 lime	$0.25	1 tablespoon dried oregano
Two 8-count packages whole-grain corn tortillas	$5.67	Salt and pepper
1 small red cabbage	$2.58	Cilantro (garden)
One 8-ounce container sour cream	$0.99	**INGREDIENTS LEFT OVER**
TOTAL	**$13.61**	N/A
COST PER SERVING	**$1.70**	

Slow Cooker Costa Rican Red Beans

Difficulty: Super easy
Prep time: 10 minutes
Cook time: 7 to 8 hours on high
Makes 3 to 4 cups
Special tools: Slow cooker

GLUTEN-FREE
DAIRY-FREE
VEGETARIAN
NUT-FREE
FREEZER-FRIENDLY

1½ cups dried red beans, rinsed

3 cups water

One 13.5-ounce can coconut milk

3 celery stalks, cut into medium dice

1 bay leaf

1 teaspoon chili powder

1 teaspoon dried thyme

1 teaspoon salt

½ teaspoon ground black pepper

My husband absolutely loves this dish, and it's super easy to make. Beans are the perfect budget-friendly ingredient to keep you feeling full. Serve this as either a side dish or the main course over brown rice with a salad (or other green veggie) to go with it.

Combine all the ingredients in a slow cooker. Cover and cook on high for 7 to 8 hours, until the beans are tender. Remove the bay leaf and serve.

SHOPPING LIST		PANTRY AND FRIDGE CHECKLIST
One 16-ounce bag dry red beans	$1.29	Bay leaf
One 13.5-ounce can coconut milk	$1.49	1 teaspoon chili powder
1 bunch celery	$2.39	1 teaspoon dried thyme
TOTAL	**$5.17**	Salt and pepper
COST PER SERVING		**INGREDIENTS LEFT OVER**
(½ cup)	**$0.65**	Red beans
		Celery

Slow Cooker Shredded Moo Shu Pork

Many moo shu recipes call for hoisin sauce, which contains sugar. As a result, since cutting out processed food, I've missed them both—I just cannot serve refined sugar for dinner. So I'm thrilled to have this more wholesome alternative, which is everything I could hope for.

1. Set the pork in a slow cooker.

2. In a medium bowl, whisk the soy sauce, peanut butter, honey, garlic, sesame oil, vinegar, and spices. Pour the mixture over the pork. Cover and cook on low for 7 to 8 hours, or until the meat is tender enough to shred easily with a fork.

Difficulty: Super easy
Prep time: 10 to 15 minutes
Cook time: 7 to 8 hours on low
Makes 6 or 8 servings (as sandwich), 4 or 6 (by itself)
Special tools: Slow cooker

GLUTEN-FREE (IF GLUTEN-FREE SOY SAUCE IS USED)
DAIRY-FREE
FREEZER-FRIENDLY

3-pound pork shoulder roast
½ cup soy sauce
¼ cup peanut butter
¼ cup honey
5 garlic cloves, minced
1 tablespoon toasted sesame oil
1 tablespoon rice vinegar
1 teaspoon ground ginger
½ teaspoon ground cinnamon
½ teaspoon ground black pepper

Suggested accompaniment to make into a "sandwich": Whole grain tortillas and shredded cabbage mix (slaw), otherwise plate with side items of choice

---

SHOPPING LIST

3 pounds pork shoulder	$9.87
One 15-ounce bottle soy sauce	$2.49
One 16-ounce jar peanut butter	$2.67
1 garlic head	$0.50
TOTAL	**$15.53**
COST PER SERVING	**$2.59**

PANTRY AND FRIDGE CHECKLIST

¼ cup honey
1 tablespoon toasted sesame oil
1 tablespoon rice vinegar
1 teaspoon ground ginger
½ teaspoon ground cinnamon
Pepper

INGREDIENTS LEFT OVER

Soy sauce
Peanut butter
Garlic

Slow Cooker Green Salsa Chicken

Difficulty: Super easy
Prep time: 5 to 10 minutes
Cook time: 3 to 4 hours on high
or 6 hours on low
Makes 6 servings
Special tools: Slow cooker

GLUTEN-FREE
DAIRY-FREE (IF OPTIONAL CHEESE
AND SOUR CREAM ARE NOT USED)
NUT-FREE
FREEZER-FRIENDLY

1½ pounds boneless skinless
chicken thighs

1 tablespoon oregano

1 teaspoon cumin

½ teaspoon salt

½ teaspoon pepper

One 15.5-ounce can pinto
beans, drained and rinsed

1½ cups frozen corn kernels

One 12-ounce jar tomatillo
salsa (I like Trader Joe's brand),
or about 1⅓ cups homemade
or other salsa verde

6 servings brown rice,
cooked according to package
directions

Suggested accompaniments:
Grated Monterey Jack cheese,
sliced avocado, sour cream,
cilantro, and/or diced jalapeño
(if you like it spicy)

This recipe is at the top of the list when it comes to quick and easy (and tasty)! Not only is there no precooking required, but there's no chopping either. You literally just dump a few items into the slow cooker, turn it on, and—voilà!—just one small set of measuring spoons to clean. And if you already have brown rice on hand (either cooked in advance or in one of those handy precooked microwavable packets), it's even easier to serve come dinnertime.

1. Place the chicken in a slow cooker and sprinkle the oregano, cumin, salt, and pepper on top. Pour in the beans, corn, and salsa and cook on high for 3 to 4 hours or low for 6 hours.

2. Spoon over the brown rice (we used 2 bags of precooked rice) and top with suggested accompaniments, if desired.

SHOPPING LIST		PANTRY AND FRIDGE CHECKLIST
1½ pounds boneless skinless chicken thighs	$4.04	1 tablespoon oregano
One 15.5-ounce can pinto beans, drained and rinsed	$0.91	1 teaspoon cumin
One 15-ounce bag frozen corn kernels	$1.69	½ teaspoon salt
One 12-ounce jar tomatillo salsa	$1.99	½ teaspoon pepper
One 16-ounce bag brown rice	$1.00	**INGREDIENTS LEFT OVER**
TOTAL	**$9.63**	Corn
COST PER SERVING	**$1.61**	Brown rice

Slow Cooker "Drumstick" Chicken Stock

Difficulty: Super easy

Prep time: 10 to 15 minutes

Cook time: 8 to 10 hours on low (for the stock)

Makes 4 to 6 quarts, depending on the size of your slow cooker

Special tools: Slow cooker

GLUTEN-FREE

DAIRY-FREE

NUT-FREE

FREEZER-FRIENDLY (AND RECOMMENDED!)

CHICKEN

5 drumsticks (weighing about 1½ pounds total)

STOCK

Chicken bones from the drumsticks (edible meat removed)

1 onion, peeled and halved

1 celery stalk, roughly chopped

1 carrot, roughly chopped (no need to peel)

1 bay leaf

1 parsley sprig

1 thyme sprig

Salt

Water (see step 3)

I've been making my own slow cooker chicken stock for years. I highly recommend it because it not only tastes much better and is better for you, but it can save you money as well! I usually make it with the leftover carcass from The Best Whole Chicken in the Slow Cooker recipe (from my first cookbook). But then one day when I was out of stock and needed it, I realized how much cheaper it would be to make stock using the bones from an inexpensive pack of drumsticks instead of breaking down and buying a box of ready-made broth. Since I almost always have onion, celery, carrot, and all the necessary spices on hand, I literally spent a little over two bucks and ended up with 6 quarts of yummy homemade stock. And a bonus—some cooked chicken from the drumsticks, too.

1. To make the chicken: Cook the drumsticks in a slow cooker according to the instructions on the opposite page.

2. To make the stock: Remove the edible meat from the drumsticks and leave everything else—including the skin, cooking juices, and original onion—in the bottom of the slow cooker.

3. Add the onion, celery, carrot, bay leaf, parsley, and thyme. Fill the slow cooker almost to the top with water (leaving at least ½ inch of headspace).

4. Cover, set to low, and cook overnight (or start the cooker in the morning and cook on low for 8 to 10 hours). If I don't have time to deal with the stock, I often leave mine going on low for days, adding more water if necessary to bring it back up to the top.

5. Using a soup ladle, pass the stock through a fine-mesh sieve to remove all the solids (discard the solids). Refrigerate the stock for 1 week or freeze in freezer-safe jars with room left at the top for the liquid to expand for up to 6 months. Dilute the stock with water (if desired) and add salt to taste before using in recipes.

The Best Whole Chicken (or Drumsticks!) in the Slow Cooker

This chicken is a staple in many of my recipes, and I love how I can even use it for an inexpensive pack of drumsticks. Peel 1 onion, cut it in half, and set it in a slow cooker. Combine 2 teaspoons paprika, 1 teaspoon salt, 1 teaspoon onion powder, 1 teaspoon dried thyme, ½ teaspoon garlic powder, ¼ teaspoon cayenne pepper, and ¼ teaspoon ground black pepper in a small bowl. Rub the spice mixture all over the chicken (or drumsticks) and place on top of the onion. Cover and cook on high for 4 hours for a whole chicken or 3 hours for drumsticks, until the chicken is falling off the bone.

SHOPPING LIST		PANTRY AND FRIDGE CHECKLIST	INGREDIENTS LEFT OVER
1½ pounds drumsticks	$3.29	Bay leaf	Celery
1 onion	$0.85	Parsley (garden)	Carrots
1 bunch celery	$2.39	Thyme (garden)	
One 1-pound bag carrots	$0.99	Salt	
TOTAL	**$7.52**		
COST PER SERVING (1 cup)	**$0.32**		

CHAPTER 8

special treats

special treat recipes

Strawberry (Whole Wheat) Shortcake

If you're looking for a dessert that's easy to make and not overly sweet, this is your answer! It's simple enough for a child to take charge of in the kitchen and calls for such a small amount of sweetener that I'm not sure it's even technically dessert. But we'll keep that between us.

1. To make the shortcakes: Preheat the oven to 450°F.

2. In a large bowl, use a fork to whisk the pastry flour, baking powder, baking soda, and salt. Pour in the maple syrup and cream and stir to combine just until the dry ingredients are moistened.

3. Pick up the dough with your hands and set it on a floured surface. Fold the dough over itself, flattening it down each time, about two dozen times. Pat it into a big square about 1 inch thick, using extra flour if necessary to keep it from sticking to your hands.

4. Use the 2-inch cookie cutter to cut the dough into 8 to 10 rounds. Place on a large baking sheet 1 to 2 inches apart and bake until golden brown, 12 to 14 minutes.

5. Meanwhile, make the topping: Pour the cream and maple syrup into a jar with a tight-fitting lid. Shake until you no longer hear liquid hitting the sides and the product looks like whipped cream. (Or you can use an electric mixer to whip the cream.)

6. To serve, split a shortcake in half horizontally. Set the bottom half on a small plate and top with a dollop of the whipped cream, some sliced strawberries, the top half of the shortcake, more whipped cream, and a handful of strawberries. Serve immediately.

Difficulty: Easy
Prep time: 15 minutes
Baking time: 12 to 14 minutes (hands-off)
Makes 8 to 10 servings
Special tools: 2-inch cookie cutter, baking sheet, and jar with tight-fitting lid or electric mixer (for the whipped cream)

VEGETARIAN
NUT-FREE
FREEZER-FRIENDLY (SHORTCAKES ONLY, WITHOUT TOPPINGS)

SHORTCAKES

2 cups whole wheat pastry flour, plus more for patting out the dough

2 teaspoons baking powder

¼ teaspoon baking soda

½ teaspoon salt

3 tablespoons pure maple syrup

1¼ cups heavy cream

TOPPING

1½ cups heavy cream

1 tablespoon pure maple syrup

1 pint fresh strawberries, hulled and thinly sliced

SHOPPING LIST

One 3-pound bag whole wheat pastry (or regular) flour	$3.69	
1½ pints heavy cream	$5.33	
1 pint strawberries	$3.00	

TOTAL	**$12.02**	
COST PER SERVING	**$1.50**	

PANTRY AND FRIDGE CHECKLIST

2 teaspoons baking powder
¼ teaspoon baking soda
Salt
¼ cup pure maple syrup

INGREDIENTS LEFT OVER

Whole wheat flour
Heavy cream

Piña Colada Frozen Yogurt Pops

Difficulty: Super easy
Prep time: 10 minutes
Freeze time: 4 to 5 hours (hands-off)
Makes 10 pops (about ¼ cup each)
Special tools: Blender, ice-pop molds, and wooden ice-pop sticks

GLUTEN-FREE
VEGETARIAN
FREEZER-FRIENDLY
NUT-FREE

1 cup plain yogurt

1 cup coconut milk (shake the can before opening and stir before using)

1 cup frozen pineapple

⅓ cup pure maple syrup

There's nothing like escaping to the tropics (mentally, at least!) with the taste of a piña colada—my all-time favorite frozen drink. Unfortunately these days many tiki bars rely on dreaded processed mixes made with high-fructose corn syrup to make their drinks. It's too bad because it's so simple to make a real (virgin) piña colada from scratch. All it takes is some pineapple and coconut milk really! This recipe turns a favorite adult beverage into a frozen yogurt pop for the whole family.

Blend all the ingredients together until smooth. Pour into ice-pop molds, insert a wooden stick into the center of each, and freeze for 4 to 5 hours or overnight.

SHOPPING LIST		PANTRY AND FRIDGE CHECKLIST
Two 5.3-ounce containers plain yogurt	$2.00	N/A
One 13.5-ounce can coconut milk	$1.49	
Oe 16-ounce bag frozen pineapple chunks	$3.59	**INGREDIENTS LEFT OVER**
One 8-ounce jar pure maple syrup	$4.99	Coconut milk
		Pineapple
TOTAL	**$12.07**	Maple syrup
COST PER SERVING	**$1.21**	

Watermelon Mint Pops

Watermelon is the top budget-friendly fruit, so it's worth being creative and finding more ways to use it in the kitchen. Aside from eating it by itself, it's great topped with chili powder and lime (page 147), mixed into a salad, or blended into these creamy mint pops.

Blend all the ingredients together until smooth. Pour into ice-pop molds, insert a wooden stick into the center of each, and freeze for 4 to 5 hours or overnight.

Difficulty: Super easy
Prep time: 10 minutes
Freeze time: 4 to 5 hours (hands-off)
Makes 10 pops (about ¼ cup each)
Special tools: Blender, ice-pop molds, and wooden ice-pop sticks

GLUTEN-FREE
DAIRY-FREE
VEGETARIAN
NUT-FREE
FREEZER-FRIENDLY

5 cups diced watermelon

1 tablespoon honey

1 tablespoon chopped fresh mint

SHOPPING LIST		PANTRY AND FRIDGE CHECKLIST
1 medium seedless watermelon	$6.99	1 tablespoon honey
		Mint (garden)
TOTAL	$6.99	
COST PER SERVING	$0.64	INGREDIENTS LEFT OVER
		Watermelon

Dark Chocolate Crumb Bars

Difficulty: Medium
Prep time: 20 minutes
Cook time: 35 to 45 minutes
   (mostly hands-off)
Makes 16 bars
Special tools: Electric mixer
   and 8 x 8-inch baking dish

VEGETARIAN
FREEZER-FRIENDLY

CRUST

1 stick (4 ounces) butter, at
room temperature, plus more
for greasing the baking dish
2 tablespoons honey or pure
maple syrup
¼ teaspoon salt
1 cup whole wheat flour

TOPPING

4 ounces unsweetened
chocolate baking bar (100%
cacao), broken into chunks
½ cup honey or pure maple
syrup
¼ teaspoon salt
½ teaspoon pure vanilla
extract
½ cup chopped raw walnuts or
pecans

Any chocolate chip cookie fan will be fond of this chocolaty dessert! It's perfect for sharing with a crowd.

1. Preheat the oven to 350°F. Grease an 8 x 8-inch baking dish with butter.

2. To make the crust: In a bowl, with an electric mixer, cream the butter until smooth, then beat in the honey and salt until well combined. Mix in the flour until the dough comes together.

3. Set aside ¼ cup of the dough and press the rest in an even layer over the bottom of the baking dish. Bake until the crust is darkened in color but not browned, 10 to 12 minutes.

4. Meanwhile, make the topping: In a small saucepan, combine the chocolate, honey, and salt and melt over very low heat. Stir in the vanilla and remove from the heat.

5. Place the nuts in a small bowl. Add the reserved ¼ cup dough and 2 tablespoons of the chocolate mixture and stir until well combined.

6. Pour the remaining chocolate mixture over the hot crust and use a spatula to spread it into an even layer. Sprinkle the walnut mixture on top.

7. Return to the oven and bake until the edges are set, 17 to 20 minutes. Cool and cut into 16 bars. Serve or store at room temperature for 3 to 4 days.

LISA'S TIP: You can double this recipe in a 9 x 13-inch baking dish for just a couple bucks more!

SHOPPING LIST

One 8-ounce box butter $2.69
One 12-ounce jar honey $2.50
One 2-pound bag whole
  wheat flour $3.49
One 4-ounce unsweetened
  chocolate baking bar
  (100% cacao) $2.24

One 4-ounce bag chopped
  walnuts $2.99
TOTAL **$13.91**
COST PER SERVING **$0.87**

PANTRY AND FRIDGE CHECKLIST

Salt
½ teaspoon pure vanilla extract

INGREDIENTS LEFT OVER

Butter
Honey
Flour

Blueberry Lemon Cheesecake

Blueberry and lemon taste great together, and this cheesecake is no exception. This dish does take a little time to make, but it's definitely worth the effort.

1. Preheat the oven to 375°F.

2. To make the crust: In a food processor, process the pecans and salt to the consistency of coarse crumbs (or chop by hand). Mix in the butter until the crust mixture comes together.

3. Using wet fingers, press the crust mixture in an even layer on the bottom and sides of a deep-dish pie plate. Bake until the crust turns a rich brown, 15 to 17 minutes. Set aside to cool. Leave the oven on and reduce the temperature to 350°F.

4. Meanwhile, make the filling: In the bowl of an electric mixer, beat the cream cheese and honey until smooth. Beat in the eggs one at a time, then the lemon zest, mixing well after each addition.

5. Pour the cream cheese mixture into the pie crust. Return to the oven and bake until the edges of the filling are puffed and begin to brown, 30 to 35 minutes.

6. Set aside to cool, then top with the blueberries. When the cheesecake is cool enough to handle, refrigerate until well chilled, at least 3 to 4 hours.

Difficulty: Medium
Prep time: 25 to 30 minutes
Bake time: 50 to 60 minutes (mostly hands-off)
Makes 8 to 10 servings
Special tools: Food processor (not necessary, but helpful), electric mixer, and 8- or 9-inch pie plate (must be at least 1½ inches deep)

GLUTEN-FREE
VEGETARIAN
FREEZER-FRIENDLY

CRUST

2 cups raw pecans
¼ teaspoon salt
4 tablespoons (½ stick) butter, at room temperature

FILLING

Two 8-ounce packages cream cheese, at room temperature
¼ cup honey
3 eggs
2 teaspoons grated lemon zest (see Tip, opposite)

TOPPING

½ to ¾ cup frozen or fresh blueberries (no need to thaw)

SHOPPING LIST		PANTRY AND FRIDGE CHECKLIST
One 8-ounce bag raw pecans	$6.48	¼ teaspoon salt
Two 8-ounce packages cream cheese	$4.00	4 tablespoons (½ stick) butter
Half dozen eggs	$0.85	¼ cup honey
1 lemon	$0.65	**INGREDIENTS LEFT OVER**
One 10-ounce bag frozen blueberries	$3.39	Eggs
TOTAL	**$15.37**	Blueberries
COST PER SERVING	**$1.54**	Lemon (save for juicing)

Sydney's Chocolate Banana Milkshake

Difficulty: Super easy
Prep time: 5 to 10 minutes
Cook time: N/A
Makes 2 small servings
Special tools: Blender

GLUTEN-FREE
VEGETARIAN
NUT-FREE

3 bananas, frozen

1 cup heavy cream

½ teaspoon pure vanilla extract

1 tablespoon honey

2 teaspoons unsweetened cocoa powder (I used Hershey's 100% cocoa Special Dark), plus more for garnish (optional)

Thirteen-year-old Sydney wanted to write her own message about this recipe so here it is! "I was bored one day after gymnastics class and Mom asked me if I had any ideas for her book. She said she needed a chocolate dessert recipe and was stumped. I thought for a moment and was like, bingo! A milkshake! So I made the banana ice cream creamier by using cream instead of milk and added cocoa powder to make it chocolate. The results were awesome! My first try, and everyone couldn't stop drinking it!"

1. In a blender, process the bananas and cream until smooth and creamy (if it stops blending, push down with a spatula and try again).

2. Add the vanilla, honey, and cocoa and blend until smooth and creamy.

3. Pour into glasses and garnish with a sprinkle of cocoa powder (optional). Serve with straws.

SHOPPING LIST		PANTRY AND FRIDGE CHECKLIST
One 8-ounce container unsweetened cocoa powder	$3.89	½ teaspoon pure vanilla extract
3 bananas	$0.60	1 tablespoon honey
½ pint heavy cream	$2.29	2 teaspoons unsweetened cocoa powder
TOTAL	**$6.78**	**INGREDIENTS LEFT OVER**
COST PER SERVING	**$3.39**	N/A

LISA'S TIP: Freezing ripe bananas is a great way to save them from ending up in the trash. Simply remove the peel (important!), break them into thirds, and throw them into a freezerproof bag in the freezer. We add to our stash all the time and use them frequently for treats like this.

homemade staples

homemade staple recipes

Southwest Ranch Dressing

This flavorful (and somewhat spicy) dressing is a great way to add lots of personality to plain old lettuce, a simple salad, or even a wrap for lunch. We especially love it paired with the Southwest Salad (page 92).

Blend all the ingredients until smooth. Store in the fridge for up to 3 days.

Difficulty: Easy
Prep time: 10 minutes
Cook time: N/A
Makes just over 1 cup
Special tools: Blender (immersion or stand)

GLUTEN-FREE
VEGETARIAN
NUT-FREE

½ cup buttermilk

½ cup sour cream

2 small canned chipotles in adobo sauce

2 tablespoons minced fresh cilantro

2 tablespoons diced green onions (white and green parts)

2 teaspoons fresh lime juice

⅛ teaspoon salt

Ground black pepper, to taste

SHOPPING LIST		PANTRY AND FRIDGE CHECKLIST
One 16-ounce carton buttermilk	$1.19	Cilantro (garden)
One 8-ounce container sour cream	$0.99	Salt and pepper
One 7-ounce can chipotles in adobo sauce	$2.69	**INGREDIENTS LEFT OVER**
1 bunch green onions	$0.89	Buttermilk
1 lime	$0.25	Sour cream
TOTAL	**$6.01**	Chipotles in adobo sauce
COST PER SERVING (2 tablespoons)	**$0.75**	Green onions

Asian Salad Dressing

Difficulty: Super easy
Prep time: 5 to 10 minutes
Cook time: N/A
Makes about ⅓ cup
Special tools: Blender (immersion or stand)

GLUTEN-FREE (IF GLUTEN-FREE SOY SAUCE IS USED)
DAIRY-FREE
VEGETARIAN
NUT-FREE

¼ cup olive oil

2 tablespoons rice vinegar

2 teaspoons soy sauce

1 teaspoon peeled and minced fresh ginger

1 garlic clove, minced

½ teaspoon honey

It's hard not to love the flavor of the salads with the Asian dressing at the hibachi steakhouses where they cook at your table. You can enjoy those delicious flavors at home with this easy salad dressing—make one batch and have it on hand all week long!

Blend all the ingredients until smooth. Pour over salad greens or refrigerate for up to 1 week.

SHOPPING LIST	
2 ounces fresh ginger	$0.63
1 garlic head	$0.50
TOTAL	**$1.13**
COST PER SERVING (2 tablespoons)	**$0.43**

PANTRY AND FRIDGE CHECKLIST

¼ cup olive oil
2 tablespoons rice vinegar
2 teaspoons soy sauce
½ teaspoon honey

INGREDIENTS LEFT OVER
Garlic
Ginger

Lemon–Poppy Seed Vinaigrette

Typical poppy seed dressing recipes call for refined sugar, and lots of it! No need to work against what would have been a healthy salad; this version uses just one tablespoon of honey. You'll be surprised at how good it is without all that sugar.

1. Blend all the ingredients using an immersion blender or shake them up in a jar to emulsify the dressing. Store in a jar.

2. Use or refrigerate for up to 1 week (the dressing will solidify). Bring to room temperature by placing the jar in warm water, then shake again before using.

SHOPPING LIST		PANTRY AND FRIDGE CHECKLIST
1 lemon	$0.65	¼ cup olive oil
1 garlic head	$0.50	1 teaspoon poppy seeds
TOTAL	**$1.15**	1 tablespoon honey
COST PER SERVING		½ teaspoon Dijon mustard
(2 tablespoons)	**$0.29**	Salt and pepper
		INGREDIENTS LEFT OVER
		Garlic

Difficulty: Super easy
Prep time: 5 to 10 minutes
Cook time: N/A
Makes about ½ cup
Special tools: Immersion blender or jar with tight-fitting lid

GLUTEN-FREE
DAIRY-FREE
VEGETARIAN
NUT-FREE

¼ cup olive oil

2 tablespoons fresh lemon juice

1 tablespoon honey, or more to taste

1 teaspoon poppy seeds

½ teaspoon Dijon mustard

1 garlic clove, minced

Salt and ground black pepper, to taste

Easy Balsamic Vinaigrette

Difficulty: Super easy
Prep time: 5 to 10 minutes
Cook time: N/A
Makes a little more than ½ cup
Special tools: Immersion
    blender or jar with tight-
    fitting lid

GLUTEN-FREE
DAIRY-FREE
VEGETARIAN
NUT-FREE

½ cup olive oil

2 tablespoons balsamic vinegar

2 garlic cloves, minced

2 teaspoons Dijon mustard

½ teaspoon salt

½ teaspoon ground black
pepper

Skip the store-bought version with its unwanted additives like emulsifiers and refined sweeteners and go for this easy, classic recipe instead!

1. Blend all the ingredients with an immersion blender or shake them up in a jar to emulsify the dressing. Store in a jar.

2. Use or refrigerate for up to 1 week (the dressing will solidify). Bring to room temperature by placing the jar in warm water, then shake again before using.

SHOPPING LIST		PANTRY AND FRIDGE CHECKLIST
One 16-ounce bottle olive oil	$4.99	2 tablespoons balsamic vinegar
1 garlic head	$0.50	2 teaspoons Dijon mustard
TOTAL	**$5.49**	Salt and pepper
PER SERVING (2 tablespoons)	**$1.37**	**INGREDIENTS LEFT OVER** Olive oil Garlic

Green Goddess Dressing

If your salads are getting a little predictable and boring, here's the perfect dressing to jazz things up! It's also fabulous drizzled over leftover chicken and lettuce on a whole wheat wrap or used as a dip for fresh veggies.

With a blender, process all the ingredients until smooth (be sure the garlic gets blended!). Serve immediately or refrigerate for up to 5 days. Shake before each use.

Difficulty: Easy
Prep time: 5 to 10 minutes
Cook time: N/A
Makes about 1¼ cups
Special tools: Blender (immersion or stand)

GLUTEN-FREE
VEGETARIAN
NUT-FREE

¾ cup plain yogurt

¼ cup milk

½ cup chopped green onions, white and green parts

½ cup loosely packed flat-leaf parsley

½ cup loosely packed basil leaves

1 garlic clove, smashed or minced

2 tablespoons fresh lemon juice

½ teaspoon salt

SHOPPING LIST			PANTRY AND FRIDGE CHECKLIST
Two 5.3-ounce containers plain yogurt		$2.00	¼ cup milk
1 bunch green onions		$0.89	Parsley (garden)
1 garlic head		$0.50	Basil (garden)
1 lemon		$0.65	Salt
TOTAL		**$4.04**	
COST PER SERVING (2 tablespoons)		**$0.40**	**INGREDIENTS LEFT OVER**
			Green onions
			Garlic
			Yogurt

Quick Fridge Pickles (Quickles)

Difficulty: Super easy
Prep time: 5 to 10 minutes
Cook time: Less than 5 minutes
Makes 2 pints
Special tools: 2 pint jars

GLUTEN-FREE
DAIRY-FREE
VEGETARIAN
NUT-FREE

1 cucumber, trimmed, halved crosswise, and cut lengthwise into long wedges
1 cup distilled white vinegar
¼ cup honey
3 garlic cloves, minced
1 teaspoon dried dill
¼ teaspoon salt
1 cup water

Anyone who grows their own veggies in the summer is always looking for ways to use up cucumbers. Here's an easy way to turn them into tasty homemade pickles without having to process or can them.

1. Divide the cucumbers between the 2 pint jars and set aside.

2. In a small saucepan, combine the vinegar, honey, garlic, dill, salt, and water. Bring to a boil over high heat.

3. Divide the liquid between the 2 jars and add more water as needed to cover the cucumbers.

4. Seal with lids, let cool, and store in the fridge for up to 1 month. They're ready to eat the following day but will be more flavorful over time.

SHOPPING LIST		PANTRY AND FRIDGE CHECKLIST
1 cucumber	$0.50	¼ cup honey
One 16-ounce bottle distilled white vinegar	$0.99	1 teaspoon dried dill
1 garlic head	$0.50	Salt
TOTAL	**$1.99**	**INGREDIENTS LEFT OVER**
COST PER SERVING		Distilled white vinegar
(2 or 3 pieces)	**$0.50**	Garlic

The Best-Ever Steak Butter

This steak butter recipe is inspired by my first-ever job in the food world. I was sixteen, full of energy, and super excited to be working as a hostess at the Chop House in Knoxville, Tennessee, where I grew up. I ended up working there for years, and when I told my husband I was making a recipe inspired by their steak butter, he said, "Well, how do you know it's the best ever?" I said, "Because it's more than twenty years later and I'm still thinking about it!" So there you go. Try it out and judge for yourself.

In a mini food processor, combine all the ingredients and blend until smooth. Smear over warm steaks and serve, or store in an airtight container in the fridge for 1 to 2 weeks.

Difficulty: Super easy
Prep time: 5 to 10 minutes
Cook time: N/A
Makes 4 servings
Special tools: Mini food processor

GLUTEN-FREE
VEGETARIAN
NUT-FREE
FREEZER-FRIENDLY

6 tablespoons butter, at room temperature

1 tablespoon chopped flat-leaf parsley leaves

1 teaspoon fresh lemon juice

½ teaspoon lemon-pepper seasoning

⅛ teaspoon ground black pepper

⅛ teaspoon salt

SHOPPING LIST		PANTRY AND FRIDGE CHECKLIST
One 8-ounce box butter (2 sticks)	$2.69	Parsley (garden)
1 lemon	$0.65	½ teaspoon lemon-pepper seasoning
TOTAL	**$3.34**	Salt and pepper
COST PER SERVING	**$0.84**	**INGREDIENTS LEFT OVER**
		Butter

"We like to have corn on the cob with our steak, and this butter is delicious on the corn, too!"

—Emily Allen, recipe tester

Easy Orange Beurre Blanc Sauce

Difficulty: Super easy
Prep time: Less than 5 minutes
Cook time: 5 to 10 minutes
Makes a generous 1 cup

GLUTEN-FREE
VEGETARIAN
NUT-FREE

½ cup dry white wine
(such as Sauvignon Blanc or
Pinot Grigio)
½ cup fresh orange juice
(about 2 oranges)
¼ cup heavy cream
6 tablespoons butter

This may sound fancy, but it's as easy as can be and super tasty poured over white fish or chicken. This one may count as a small splurge, but would be a great way to switch up dinner!

1. In a small skillet, whisk the wine, orange juice, and cream over medium-high heat until the ingredients come together. Reduce the heat and simmer until the liquid is reduced by about half, 5 to 10 minutes.

2. Stir in the butter until melted. Serve warm, poured over fish or chicken. Refrigerate leftovers for up to 5 days.

SHOPPING LIST		PANTRY AND FRIDGE CHECKLIST
1 bottle* dry white wine	$4.99	N/A
2 oranges	$2.98	
½ pint heavy cream	$2.29	**INGREDIENTS LEFT OVER**
One 8-ounce box butter (2 sticks)	$2.69	White wine
TOTAL	**$12.95**	Orange juice
COST PER SERVING (¼ cup)	**$3.24**	Heavy cream
		Butter

*Or look for a small single-serve bottle or Tetra Pak if you don't plan to enjoy the leftovers.

Hot Ginger Tea

Inspired by my sweet friend Catherine McCord of Weelicious (and her website and cookbooks), this is my go-to drink when we're fighting any kind of sore throat or cold. I'm not a huge fan of teabag tea, but I do love this fresh recipe when I need it most.

Add the ginger to the hot water, cover, and steep for a few minutes. Strain out the ginger and add the lemon juice and honey. Stir and serve warm.

Difficulty: Super easy
Prep time: 5 to 10 minutes
Cook time: N/A
Makes 1 serving

GLUTEN-FREE
DAIRY-FREE
VEGETARIAN
NUT-FREE

1 cup hot water
¼ teaspoon minced fresh ginger (or shave a piece with a vegetable peeler)
½ teaspoon fresh lemon juice
1 teaspoon honey (or to taste)

SHOPPING LIST		PANTRY AND FRIDGE CHECKLIST
1 lemon	$0.65	
2 ounces fresh ginger	$0.63	1 teaspoon honey
TOTAL	**$1.28**	**INGREDIENTS LEFT OVER**
COST PER SERVING	**$1.28**	Lemon
		Ginger

"This tea was so delicious. I was hesitant about adding ginger to a drink because I usually only use it in things like stir-fries, but I was pleasantly surprised."

—Kara Byers, recipe tester

LISA'S TIP: Whenever one of my girls feels a sore (or scratchy) throat coming on, I like to send them out the door with a cup of this in a Thermos on school mornings.

Flavored Water—Two Ways

Difficulty: Super easy
Prep time: 5 minutes
Cook time: N/A
Makes 1 serving each

GLUTEN-FREE
DAIRY-FREE
VEGETARIAN
NUT-FREE

1 cup plain sparkling water
(any variety, such as seltzer or
sparkling natural mineral water)

3 tablespoons fresh grapefruit
juice

½ teaspoon honey

How about giving up soda, for the benefit of both your health and your wallet? These homemade flavored waters may be your ticket to victory—and inspire you to create your own personal favorites!

SPARKLING GRAPEFRUIT

Mix the ingredients until well combined. Serve chilled.

SHOPPING LIST		PANTRY AND FRIDGE CHECKLIST
One 33.8-ounce bottle seltzer	$0.89	½ teaspoon honey
1 grapefruit	$1.49	**INGREDIENTS LEFT OVER**
TOTAL	**$2.38**	Seltzer
COST PER SERVING	**$2.38**	Grapefruit

8 ounces cold water
4 slices cucumber
2 big mint leaves, torn

CUCUMBER MINT

Combine the ingredients in a glass and use a straw to muddle the mint leaves at the bottom to help bring out the flavor. Serve chilled or store in the fridge for up to 3 days. The longer it sits, the more flavorful it will be.

SHOPPING LIST		PANTRY AND FRIDGE CHECKLIST
1 cucumber	$0.50	Mint (garden)
TOTAL	**$0.50**	
COST PER SERVING	**$0.50**	**INGREDIENTS LEFT OVER**
		Cucumber

LISA'S TIPS: Here's how to make a full pitcher of these flavored waters.
   Sparkling Grapefruit: Fill a pitcher with 6 cups (48 ounces) sparkling water and mix in the juice from 1 grapefruit (about 1 cup + 2 tablespoons juice) and 1 tablespoon honey.
   Cucumber Mint: Fill a pitcher with 7 cups cold water, about half a cucumber, sliced, and 14 big mint leaves (torn).

acknowledgments

It takes a village when it comes to pulling together a cookbook! I was uncertain at times if I could pull off an entire book of real food recipes "on a budget," but really wanted to make this vision a reality for all those cost-conscious readers out there, and I couldn't have done it without a wonderful support team behind me all the way!

To my husband, Jason, and daughters, Sydney and Sienna, I love you three more than you'll ever know! I could have never completed book number three (!!) without your unconditional love and support and honest feedback (even if it's sometimes not what I want to hear) on my constant recipe experiments. Thank you for being the best taste testers on the planet and for always motivating me to keep going! I am so grateful to have each of you in my life.

To my parents, for being my number one fans and always reading every article, watching every news clip, and keeping your friends (and sometimes even random strangers that may be sitting next to you on the airplane, ha ha) updated on my upcoming cookbooks and why they should buy one. Your support does not go unnoticed!

To my extended family and close friends, who always have my back. I can't imagine life without my "tribe," including Jenn, Myrtle, and our Clemson crew, Valerie, Holly, and the rest of our "playgroup" gang, and Erin (more on you below!). To Laura, Haley, and the rest of our FHS friends, for always acting like I'm a bigger deal than I really am, y'all crack me up and I love you for it. To my blogging team, who I can count on no matter what—including Kiran Dodeja Smith, Amanda Rosen, Shawn Keller, and Amy Taylor—for constant behind-the-scenes support, including occasional trips to the grocery store on a moment's notice for more pricing (you know who you are)! Kellie Brown, thank you as well for your help with all the ingredient pricing.

To my agent, Meg Thompson, for more than six years of working together in such a solid partnership . . . I absolutely love having you in my court! To my amazing and easy-to-work-with editor, Cassie Jones, for always letting me have creative control whenever necessary so my vision can become a reality. It's hard to imagine going through this process without you and the talented team at William Morrow, including Kara Zauberman, Liate Stehlik, Lynn Grady, Ryan Cury, Anwesha Basu, Rachel Meyers, Paula Szafranski, and Marta Durkin.

To the many people who helped make the photos in this book better than I could have imagined: Thank you, Erin Rutherford (pictured on page 274), for once again taking time out of your busy schedule to not only ensure we look presentable, but to even play "prop stylist" for all our photography needs. You are so talented! I loved having you, as well as Drew, Riley, and Brooks, in front of the camera with us this time.

Also, thank you, Kiran, for loaning me your precious kids, Jaiden, Deja, Shaela, and Sajin, who hammed it up for the camera at the exact right moments! I knew I could count on them to be photogenic cuties and appreciate you taking the time to get them ready and bring them over for the shoot.

Thank you to Lindsey Rose Johnson for the food photography and styling, as always, and Daniel and Candice Lanning with The Beautiful Mess for the lifestyle photography. I'm grateful to have these memories and will cherish them—I can always count on you to make my cookbooks feel like a treasured family photo album! Thank you, Tami Hardeman and Heidi Billotto, for food styling and filling in at the last minute. We wouldn't have survived the shoot without you!

To David Blackley and Pressly Williams, for allowing us to use Renfrow Hardware and Renfrow Farms for some of our beautiful backdrops in the pictures. Hard to beat your field of flowers! To the Matthews Farmers' Market (my favorite) and Whole Foods Market, for letting us shoot photos on location again as well. To Kymm McLean with Who Is the Fairest, for making sure I looked presentable enough for pictures and for giving the girls a little blush to make them feel included. To Amanda Dudzik, for making sure Sienna's hair lived up to its full potential, and to Twine & Twig and Erin at Isabella, both in Charlotte, for letting us borrow so many items for the photo shoot. Gotta love all these wonderful resources we have right here in Charlotte!

Above all else, to the amazingly loyal readers of my blog and books. Your stories inspire me every day, and I thank you for being on this journey with me.

RECIPE AND MEAL PLAN TESTERS

A huge thank-you to Meghan Alpern, for once again doing an amazing job coordinating all my recipe testers. I could not have handled this piece without you and appreciate your fitting it into your already busy schedule! And, of course, a huge thank-you to the following volunteer recipe and meal plan testers. This book would not be what it is without your invaluable input: Brittany Albrinck, Emily Allen, Melissa Anderson, Tracy Andrews, Jessica Armes, Jenny Bailey, Marissa Barashi, Andrea Becker, Thea Beers, Jen Best, Simi Bhatia, Melinda Blonshine, Elizabeth Burkhalter, Kara Byers, Heather Capistrant, Sandy Carden, Melody Carpenter, Debbie Carter, Holly Chapman, Angie Chymy, Amy Coe Goins, Sharee Collier, Sharon Collins, Lindsey Congeni, Maura Conyngham, Emily Cornett, Christine Cox, Alice Cruse, Nicole Cufaude, Ashley Cullen, Holly Cunningham, Christine Dalzell, Erin Dart, Laura Davies, Bianka DeGabrielle, Cheryl Dellinger, Jan DiMare, Theresa Diulus, Jennifer Drake, Laura Falls, Jennifer Fleming, Jessica Fletcher, Emily Flynn, Brian Foster, Jeanne Foy, Jen Fuller, Julie Gal-Or, Jennifer Gilbert, Lindsay Gilbert, Debbi Gordon, Christine Hamilton, Angela Hardcastle, Korin Harms, Susan Harris, Lee Harrison, Jennifer Hennessey, Katie Hines, Jeannie Hixson, Danielle Holliday, Jenny Horrigan, Shannon Hudson, Lillian Hughes, Rhonda Iglehart, Susan Iskowich, Marcie Jackson, Robin Jenkins, Keri Jensen, Jennifer Johansen, Carrie Johnsen, Jorgee Johnson, Kelly Johnson, Kim Johnson, Leigh Kelley, Diane Kitson, Nicole Klett, Kara Kramer-Rapp, Ashley Larsen, Jodie Larsen, Melissa Larsen, Crystal Leahy, Tonya Leininger, Beth Lome, Yvonne Lowe, Maria MacKay, Beth Macurdy, Melody Maki, Mary Mapes, Kate McComb, Amber Mcdonald, Lily McGavin, Stephanie McGoldrick, Sara Corinne McLarin-Hadden, Sydney McMillan, Jennifer Mechling, Richelle Melseaux, Marion Millan, Angela Miller, Eileen Miller, Miranda Miller, Jennifer Moon, Summer Morrell, Lori Mucci, Karen Murphy, Lauren Neybert, Cinda O'Keefe, Monica Ochoa, Cassandra Oravecz, Katie Peterson, Kim Pieplow, Kirsten Pope, Kim Powell, Eleanor Preston, Samantha Quaderer, Angie Raake, Shari Ramsey, Janelle Reese, Andrea Renaud-Blonde, Kim Robert, Emma Robin, Jolene Roosekrans, Mary Rosewood, Mary Ruetten, Jen Russell, Rachel Sanders, Sheila Sandford, Melissa Schabel, Melanie Shank, Sherri Shorter, Ginny Smith, Chandra Smolen, Jennifer Snider, Amy Solak, Anne Sparks, Kimberli Spolar, LeeAnn Steward, Chasity Stricklin, Megan Stupak, Kallie Sulanke, Tracy Suykerbuyk, Laura Tapken, Abbey Temple, Carly Tucker, Leslie Tutty, Barb Umland, Valerie Urnis, Emily Waller, Claudia Walter, Courtney Warner, Ellen Wasson, Teresa Wegesser, Carrie Welker, Laura Whetstone, Emily Wilkins, Amy Wirt, and Marissa Wolfe.

notes

Chapter 1: Budgeting Tips and Resources

1. Michael Pollan, *In Defense of Food: An Eater's Manifesto* (Penguin Press, 2008), page 166.

2. The Environmental Working Group, "Dirty Dozen, EWG's 2018 Shopper's Guide to Pesticides in Produce," https://www.ewg.org/foodnews/dirty-dozen.php.

3. High-risk GMO crops: Non-GMO Project, "What Is GMO?," www.nongmoproject.org/learn-more/what-is-gmo/.

4. Brad Plumer, "How the United States Manages to Waste $165 Billion in Food Per Year," *Washington Post*, August 22, 2012, https://www.washingtonpost.com/news/wonk/wp/2012/08/22/how-food-actually-gets-wasted-in-the-united-states/.

universal conversion chart

OVEN TEMPERATURE EQUIVALENTS

250°F = 120°C

275°F = 135°C

300°F = 150°C

325°F = 160°C

350°F = 180°C

375°F = 190°C

400°F = 200°C

425°F = 220°C

450°F = 230°C

475°F = 240°C

500°F = 260°C

MEASUREMENT EQUIVALENTS

Measurements should always be level unless directed otherwise.

⅛ teaspoon = 0.5 mL

¼ teaspoon = 1 mL

½ teaspoon = 2 mL

1 teaspoon = 5 mL

1 tablespoon = 3 teaspoons = ½ fluid ounce = 15 mL

2 tablespoons = ⅛ cup = 1 fluid ounce = 30 mL

4 tablespoons = ¼ cup = 2 fluid ounces = 60 mL

5⅓ tablespoons = ⅓ cup = 3 fluid ounces = 80 mL

8 tablespoons = ½ cup = 4 fluid ounces = 120 mL

10⅔ tablespoons = ⅔ cup = 5 fluid ounces = 160 mL

12 tablespoons = ¾ cup = 6 fluid ounces = 180 mL

16 tablespoons = 1 cup = 8 fluid ounces = 240 mL

cookbook recipe chart by dietary need

Always double-check recipes/ingredients for potential allergens and review noted substitutions.

	GLUTEN-FREE	DAIRY-FREE	VEGETARIAN	PEANUT/TREE-NUT-FREE	FREEZER-FRIENDLY	PAGE NUMBER
Breakfast						
The Best Waffles			✓	✓	✓	55
Breakfast Smoothie Bowl	✓[1]	✓	✓	✓[2]	✓[3]	56
Black Olive and Tomato Frittata	✓	✓	✓	✓		59
Cinnamon Roll Pancakes			✓		✓	60
Huevos Rancheros (with Shortcut "Refried" Beans)	✓		✓	✓		63
Raspberry Delight Breakfast Smoothie	✓		✓	✓	✓	65
Budget Granola	✓[1]	✓[4]	✓		✓	66
Loaded Biscuits				✓	✓	69
Smoked Salmon Cakes				✓	✓	70
Zucchini Egg Scramble	✓		✓	✓		73
Apple Pie French Toast	✓[1]		✓	✓	✓	74
Packed Lunch						
Chicken Burrito Bowls	✓	✓[5]		✓		80
Pimiento Mac and Cheese			✓	✓	✓	82
Lemon Poppy Seed Muffins with Toasted Coconut			✓	✓	✓	84

	GLUTEN-FREE	DAIRY-FREE	VEGETARIAN	PEANUT/TREE-NUT-FREE	FREEZER-FRIENDLY	PAGE NUMBER
Creamy Pasta Salad with Broccoli and Raisins	✓[1]		✓	✓		87
Classic Potato Salad (Without Mayo!)	✓		✓	✓		88
Simple Zucchini Soup	✓	✓[5]	✓	✓	✓	90
Southwest Salad	✓	✓[7]	✓	✓		92
Deconstructed Spring Roll Bowls	✓[8]	✓	✓[9]			94
Portobello Tartine	✓[1]		✓	✓		96
Easy Chickpea Salad	✓	✓	✓	✓		99
Creamy Kale Caesar Salad	✓		✓			100
Smoked Salmon Wraps	✓[1]			✓		103

Salads and Sides

	GLUTEN-FREE	DAIRY-FREE	VEGETARIAN	PEANUT/TREE-NUT-FREE	FREEZER-FRIENDLY	PAGE NUMBER
My Favorite Summer Salad	✓		✓	✓		109
Rainbow Salad with Salmon	✓	✓[8]		✓		110
Green Apple–Cucumber Slaw	✓		✓	✓		113
Campfire Potatoes	✓	✓	✓	✓		114
Black Bean and Sweet Potato Cakes		✓[5]	✓	✓	✓	117
Melt-in-Your-Mouth Cream Biscuits			✓	✓	✓	118
Kale and Bacon–Stuffed Potatoes	✓			✓	✓	121
Shredded Brussels Sprouts	✓	✓[5]	✓	✓		123
Zucchini and Feta Fritters			✓	✓	✓	125
Sheet Pan Brussels Sprouts and Potatoes	✓	✓	✓	✓		126
Stir-Fry Broccoli	✓	✓	✓	✓		129
Coconut Rice	✓	✓	✓	✓	✓	130
Maple-Roasted Sweet Potatoes and Carrots	✓	✓	✓	✓		131
Cheesy Mashed Potato Casserole	✓		✓	✓	✓	132

	GLUTEN-FREE	DAIRY-FREE	VEGETARIAN	PEANUT/TREE-NUT-FREE	FREEZER-FRIENDLY	PAGE NUMBER
Snacks and Appetizers						
Oatmeal Cookie Energy Bites	✓[1]	✓	✓			139
Lemon and Feta Quinoa Cakes			✓	✓	✓	140
Flavored Toast—Three Ways	✓[1]		✓	✓		142
Easy Green Smoothie	✓	✓	✓	✓	✓	145
Chili-Lime-Watermelon Skewers	✓	✓	✓	✓		147
Whole Wheat Banana (Nut) Muffins		✓	✓	✓[10]	✓	148
Fruit Leather—Two Ways	✓	✓	✓	✓	✓	151
Easy Pickle Dip	✓		✓	✓		153
Roasted Rosemary Almonds	✓	✓	✓			155
The Best Oven-Baked Chicken Wings!	✓	✓		✓	✓	157
Simple Dinners						
The Easiest Spinach Lasagna			✓	✓	✓	163
Braised Chicken and Carrots with Rosemary Gravy				✓	✓	164
Simple Walnut-Crusted Salmon	✓[1]	✓				167
Easy Chinese Chicken		✓		✓	✓	168
Cheesy Zucchini "Meatballs"			✓	✓	✓	171
Asian Chicken Lettuce Cups	✓[8]	✓		✓		172
Sydney's Veggie Cream Pasta	✓[1]		✓	✓		175
Apple-Glazed Pork Chops				✓		176
Sausage and Pepper Tacos	✓[1]	✓		✓	✓	179
Mushroom and Brussels Sprouts Quesadillas	✓[1]		✓	✓	✓	180
Jason's Carne Asada	✓	✓		✓	✓	183
Baked Shells with Ricotta and Marinara	✓[1]		✓[6]	✓	✓	184
Fast-Food Chicken Nuggets		✓		✓	✓	186
Baked Bean-Stuffed Potatoes	✓	✓[5]		✓		188
Creamy Braised Pork Chops	✓			✓		191

	GLUTEN-FREE	DAIRY-FREE	VEGETARIAN	PEANUT/TREE-NUT-FREE	FREEZER-FRIENDLY	PAGE NUMBER
Cheesy Eggplant Bake	✓		✓	✓	✓	192
Sienna's Chicken and Sweet Potato Quesadillas	✓			✓	✓	194
Spaghetti Squash Carbonara	✓			✓	✓	196
Teriyaki Beef Skewers	✓[8]	✓			✓	199
Easy Chicken Scaloppine		✓			✓	200
Quick and Easy Fried Rice	✓[8]	✓	✓	✓		203
Swedish Meatballs				✓	✓	204
Oven-Baked Sweet Potato Taquitos	✓		✓	✓	✓	207
Weeknight Tandoori Chicken	✓	✓[5]		✓	✓	208
Zucchini and Black Bean Enchiladas	✓		✓	✓	✓	211
Breadcrumb-Roasted Chicken				✓	✓	212

Slow Cooker Favorites

	GLUTEN-FREE	DAIRY-FREE	VEGETARIAN	PEANUT/TREE-NUT-FREE	FREEZER-FRIENDLY	PAGE NUMBER
Slow Cooker Cuban Pork	✓[8]	✓[8]		✓	✓	219
Slow Cooker Mongolian Beef	✓[8]	✓		✓	✓	220
Slow Cooker Carrot Curry Soup	✓	✓[5]	✓[6]		✓	223
Slow Cooker Pulled Chicken Tacos	✓	✓[8]		✓	✓	224
Slow Cooker Costa Rican Red Beans	✓	✓	✓	✓	✓	226
Slow Cooker Shredded Moo Shu Pork	✓[8]	✓			✓	229
Slow Cooker Green Salsa Chicken	✓	✓[5]		✓	✓	230
Slow Cooker "Drumstick" Chicken Stock	✓	✓		✓	✓	232

Special Treats

	GLUTEN-FREE	DAIRY-FREE	VEGETARIAN	PEANUT/TREE-NUT-FREE	FREEZER-FRIENDLY	PAGE NUMBER
Strawberry (Whole Wheat) Shortcake			✓	✓	✓[12]	239
Piña Colada Frozen Yogurt Pops	✓		✓		✓	240
Watermelon Mint Pops	✓	✓	✓	✓	✓	243
Dark Chocolate Crumb Bars			✓		✓	244
Blueberry Lemon Cheesecake	✓		✓		✓	247
Sydney's Chocolate Banana Milkshake	✓		✓	✓		248

	GLUTEN-FREE	DAIRY-FREE	VEGETARIAN	PEANUT/TREE-NUT-FREE	FREEZER-FRIENDLY	PAGE NUMBER
Homemade Staples						
Southwest Ranch Dressing	✓		✓	✓		255
Asian Salad Dressing	✓[8]	✓	✓	✓		256
Lemon–Poppy Seed Vinaigrette	✓	✓	✓	✓		259
Easy Balsamic Vinaigrette	✓	✓	✓	✓		260
Green Goddess Dressing	✓		✓	✓		263
Quick Fridge Pickles (Quickles)	✓	✓	✓	✓		264
The Best-Ever Steak Butter	✓		✓	✓	✓	267
East Orange Beurre Blanc Sauce	✓		✓	✓		268
Hot Ginger Tea	✓	✓	✓	✓		271
Flavored Water—Two Ways	✓	✓	✓	✓		272

NOTES:

1. Use gluten-free bread/pita/crackers/noodles/tortillas/breadcrumbs/oats as appropriate.

2. Omit the peanut butter.

3. If thawed slightly to return original consistency before eating.

4. Substitute coconut oil for butter.

5. Omit sour cream, butter, yogurt, and/or cheese.

6. Use vegetable broth.

7. If vinaigrette is used.

8. Use gluten-free soy sauce.

9. Omit the shrimp.

10. Omit the walnuts.

11. Omit sandwich fixings.

12. Shortcakes only, without toppings.

*Most people who are allergic to tree nuts can safely eat coconut, but talk to your allergist before consuming.

index

Note: Page references in *italics* indicate photographs.